WORKING WITH PATIENTS
Introductory Guidelines
for Psychotherapists

WORKING WITH PATIENTS
Introductory Guidelines
for Psychotherapists

Helen De Rosis, M.D.

with a Foreword by
Lawrence C. Kolb, M.D.

AGATHON PRESS, INC.
New York

Agathon Press, Inc.
150 Fifth Avenue
New York, N. Y. 10011

Library of Congress Cataloging in Publication Data

De Rosis, Helen.
  Working with patients.

  Includes index.
  1. Psychoanalysis.   I.   Title.
RC504.D387   616.8:914   77-896
ISBN 0-87586-057-5

Printed in the United States

To My Mother

Contents

Foreword

In his *Art of Teaching,* Gilbert Highet stated that students learn far better by the tutorial method of education than by the lecture and recitation method. In the technique described by Highet, the tutor comes to know his students extraordinarily well, often better than their parents know them. His questions and suggestions steer the pupil slowly and imperceptibly—with frequent failures and digressions—toward where the truths rest, and the student is required to think through toward those goals.

With extraordinary perception, Highet compared the tutorial system of education to the role of the psychoanalyst with his patient. An equally or even more valid comparison might be made to the role of the supervisor of the beginning psychotherapist—a role that originally evolved out of the work of psychoanalytic institutes as they developed procedures for training psychoanalysts. These supervisory techniques were broadly adopted by many university and hospital departments of psychiatry in this country, where in the last several decades the attempt has been made to teach psychodynamic psychotherapy.

Dr. Helen DeRosis is a product of this system of tutorial teaching. She early dedicated herself to learning the theory and techniques of dynamic psychiatry, and then psychoanalysis. In recent years, she in turn has been passing on her knowledge and experience to those who aspire, as she did, to help alleviate the suffering that results from behavioral disorders due to emotional disturbance. Entrants to this field of endeavor will find in this book a documentation of the numerous problems that in her experience generally face the beginning psychotherapist. They will also find first-hand practical advice concerning the human approaches that help solve these problems as one works with patients.

During her years of practice and clinical teaching, Helen DeRosis has experienced and clearly noted with her students many of the difficulties that are encountered in this unique learning process. She comments on the limiting preconceptions and assumptions that beginners bring to their initial therapeutic encounters, misconceptions built up from the hearsay that derives from passive listening in conversational exchanges, in lectures and from book learning. She is most sensitive to the need for searching out and encouraging the positive assets of the patient as well as the intuitive insights of the beginning psychotherapist. Her long experience will provide her readers with pragmatic advice on the vicissitudes of the doctor-patient alliance, on working with the suicide threatener and the potential acter-out of violence, and some of the ways and means of working with parents and family.

All those interested in psychotherapy, beginners as well as supervisors, will find much of value in this work.

Lawrence C. Kolb, M.D.

Preface

In a sense, human beings are "overqualified" for existence on this earth. As technology seems to have advanced beyond man's capacity to have it serve him only as a constructive force, man's intellectual achievements have, in too many areas, outdistanced his ability to derive joy and fulfillment from their fruits. A modicum of intelligence is required for survival. Unless man harnesses his capacities to some form of useful and/or satisfying occupation, in compatible concert with his fellows, he is sooner or later driven to contemplate the sterility of so many man-made importances. The experiencing of existence may be one of profound joy with an infinite capacity for reaching out, or one of tethered groping in a world of "little boxes."

Insistent tottering on the edge of a void drives one to seek facsimile lifelines through a variety of stimulants—overwork, overindulgence in drugs, sex, food, travel, sports, education, art, etc. Those farthest from the abyss content themselves without resorting to extremes. The mark of wholeness is the ability to join in and to enjoy fully or to withdraw for solitude and contemplation, when desire or occasion warrants.

Man's wisdom permits him to sense the infinite variety inherent in his existence. Feeling that he is unable to take into stride such riches, he may become anxiety ridden. He must then elaborate defenses to protect himself from maddening uncertainty and corrosive self-hate. To deprive him of those defenses is the ultimate unkindness—whatever its intent.

In another lifetime of constructive growth, one might transcend the need for such defenses. That goal is beyond the young trainee in a short-term treatment situation. However, much can be done to relieve the patient. Basic concepts are presented here to help the tyro therapist provide such assistance.

One of the difficulties in teaching beginners is that experienced therapists sometimes lose sight of the problem of dealing with mundane basics confronting and confounding inexperienced workers. The latter may then be overloaded with observations and suggestions that, though valid, are too complex for their level of development.

This volume aims at both avoiding the making of that error and providing the beginner with workable first steps to guide his progress as psychotherapist. Garden-variety misconceptions are pointed out and areas for treading gingerly or courageously are indicated. Emphasis is placed on judicious use of whatever resources the therapist brings to his work. General principles of emotional disturbances are underscored in the context of hostility, depression, suicide, anxiety, conflict, and other common symptomatology. Stress is placed on the value of viewing the patient not as a mass of total illness but as a person with elements of health obscured by pathology. Throughout are scattered suggestions for specific procedures, referring to the what and how of technique and responding to the questions: "You've told me what I should try to do, but how do I do it?"; "What do I say to the patient, and when do I say it?" It is always for the therapist, however, to determine if, how, and when any suggestions are to be applied.

Chapters 1 to 14 are revised versions of papers that appeard in *The Psychiatric Quarterly* (published by the New York State Deparment of Mental Health) between 1967 and 1974.

Acknowledgments

The many students with whom I have worked are the ones I want particularly to thank for providing me with repeated opportunities to elaborate and test the approaches I have felt to be useful to the beginner. These students have been psychiatric residents and other mental health workers at The Roosevelt Hospital, and candidates-in-training at the American Institute for Psychoanalysis, both in New York City. I also want to thank Mr. Austin Smith, Assistant Editor of the *Psychiatric Quarterly,* where many of these papers first appeared, for his consistent, courteous help in the preparation of the original manuscripts for publication. To Mr. Abe Leeman goes my gratitude for initially suggesting that I prepare the collection in one volume. I am Grateful to my colleagues at the hospital and the institute for the opportunity and great pleasure of working with trainees.

Helen De Rosis

WORKING WITH PATIENTS
Introductory Guidelines
for Psychotherapists

CHAPTER I

Accentuate the Positive

Hospitalized Patient

It is a well-known fact that in a hospital setting the most severely ill patients are treated by the least experienced therapists. However, because of a generally therapeutic milieu provided by hospital facilities and staff, such lack of experience has not, in most cases, appeared to be damaging to the patient. Indeed, there have been innumerable instances where the response of the hospitalized patient has been stimulated by the ministrations of inexperienced psychotherapists.

There are many factors responsible for that. They have to do with a quality of being, with enthusiasm, optimism and possibly with an ability to keep one's mouth shut. Even when a therapist *desires* to keep it shut completely, he can still depend upon his failure to do so. What he does say can then be enough to establish the kind of rapport between patient and therapist which indicates to the patient that someone is interested in him and accepts him as he is. This, of course, is the single most significant therapeutic service that the inexperienced therapist can offer a generally bereft, isolated patient. Technique acquired in further training merely refines and makes therapeutically effective this basic encounter of interest and acceptance.

This is not to say, however, that technique is not important. There is a great need to develop techniques to serve a patient most effectively. Such questions as "What should be done first?"; "What should be left unmolested?"; "What should be said or left unsaid?" are repeatedly raised.

These questions are raised throughout one's career, and must be answered thoughtfully with each new patient. But the novice raises them with some anxiety for he often feels unequal to his assigned task. For him, there remains much ambiguity about the answers.

Still other questions arise: Is it possible for the beginning psychotherapist to learn anything of significance in the first month or in the first year of his training that will be of any practical use to him in the treatment of his patient? Does he have to rely upon the therapeutic thrust of combined departments of an institution in order to feel that his patient has benefited from a stay in the hospital?

I believe there are procedures which will assist the worker in organizing his psychotherapeutic intervention in such a way that it will be more effective than formerly. The procedures to be described here have been repeatedly outlined and discussed in supervision hours with inexperienced therapists, and have been found to provide some useful guidelines for the beginning therapist.

No Psychoanalysis

The inpatient and outpatient populations of a psychiatric facility usually consist of the most severely ill persons, where perhaps 75% of the diagnoses fall into the category of the schizophrenic reactions. It has to be stated. therefore, that while the suggestions made here *may* apply to psychoanalytic procedures used in the private office, the reverse is not necessarily the case. In all probability, traditional psychoanalytic theory and practice may *not* be applied directly to this kind of patient.

This is another way of saying that the psychoanalytic patient is one of a select group which, in the context of all individuals requiring psychiatric intervention, is very small indeed. Rarely does the hospitalized patient fall into this small group. That does not mean that he may not, at some time, be greatly helped by psychotherapy administered by a therapist who is well-schooled in psychoanalytic concepts.

While discussion pertaining to analytic theory frequently arises in supervision, theories and techniques discussed are more for academic enlightenment than for application, undiluted, to the hospitalized patient. Often it becomes necessary to state categorically to the tyro therapist, "You may believe that your patient wants to return to his mother's womb, but how would it help him to discuss his dependency in those terms? Is it, further, of any help to him to discuss his dependency at all? Or might this only add to an already abiding sense of inadequacy as a human being? If you do insist, however, upon discussing this point with him, and he finally agrees with you, what does he do then? Does he try to climb back in, or does he remain forever frustrated and furious that this is impossible?"

Young therapists are generally pleased at discovering in the patient what they identify as the oedipal conflict. In that case a supervisor is justified in remarking, "You're right, the patient was never able to resolve his wish to take his mother away from his father. Do you think he will resolve it now under your tutelage?"

If a patient must resume living with parents, or even just see them from time to time, how helpful is this information going to be to him? How does he regard his mother whom he is supposed to want to take away? How does he regard his father as his competitor?

It must be remembered that in many of these patients we are dealing with a probable schizophrenic process. How much ego strength is available? Does this patient have the same degree of intactness and the same effective defenses that the psychoanalytic patient usually has? Even though the relatively healthy analytic patient sometimes profits from an exploration of oedipal conflicts, can this approach have any relevance to the poorly integrated patient? Does such an approach further burden the hospitalized patient in his confusedly complicated relationship with his parents; or does it help him to reduce the tensions and to make being with them more comfortable? If the latter is the case then the approach is justifiable. In the early training period, however, it has not been found that these approaches are useful. In fact, they can make for even greater confusion and disintegration than before. Many experienced workers have found this out for themselves, but the inexperienced one has no way of knowing this. He must be repeatedly reminded of it, and must be given other tools with which to work.

What Cures?

It is an interesting speculation to consider the treatment of the mentally ill patient without once referring to his pathology. I do not know if that would be effective. I do know, however, that treatment is sometimes conducted by almost exclusive reference to the patient's pathology. This is particularly true in group therapy. The reference to one or another group member's "symptoms" or "compulsive drives" or "resistances" becomes a kind of *home base* with which both patient and therapist feel comfortable, familiar—sometimes even cozy. This *raison d'être* for people to be together in an accepting, nonisolating situation is not apt to be given up easily. Even though one may recognize that the positive features of the group's meeting are conducive to a therapeutic outcome, isn't it possible that greater effectiveness might obtain if reference to pathology were not the main emphasis of the group process.

What, then, is to be the content of a therapeutic session, whether individual or group? Undoubtedly, pathology will be talked about. But it would seem that equal or greater emphasis might be placed upon talking about and/or experiencing the healthy features of the patient's character structure, environment, and development. To discover, identify, and describe these features may take greater skill than to deal with pathology. The pathology is lying all about. A third-year medical student can describe this with ease for any given patient and can engage the patient in a running discussion of it.

But just how does that help the patient? Does the hospitalized patient recover from the onslaught of the disease process which hospitalized him in the first place because he has talked about his illness at great length? Or does he recover because he has (1) interrupted the associative patterns with significant persons in his environment, or (2) been exposed to a new set of experiences, persons, activities, or (3) had the opportunity to see himself able to respond in ways other than his "sick" ones, or (4) had the opportunity to relate to relatively well persons and been sincerely received by them for perhaps the first time in his life? The latter points are certainly no less significant than references to the patient's pathology, if indeed that is helpful at all. A ten-year open-ward study directed at Yale by Drs. Detre and Tucker is a strong argument in favor of underscoring the strength of the patient, rather than his pathology.

Islands of Health

How does the first-year trainee go about underscoring the strengths of his patient? How does he identify a strength in the first place? How does he make use of it, once he has found it? Any description of an area in his life that has been of interest, pleasure, or satisfaction to the patient usually depicts a strength. Those areas do not have to include success at school, on the athletic field, in business, love, marriage, or any of the other conventional yardsticks that are automatically used to measure success. In fact, the patient may never have had success in any of these areas. Then what have his satisfactions been? Does this mean he is left without anything positive to speak of? Not very likely, if the therapist is open to hearing and picking up such points when and as they arise in the therapeutic session.

Thus, a passive, dependent, depressed, isolated, mild, fifty-seven-year-old man, unmarried, with a long-standing diagnosis of multiple sclerosis, had very little to say about his rather narrow, constricted life in which there seemed to be no bright moments whatsoever. He had been successful in none of the conventional areas. When he was asked about his work as a cutter in a garment firm, he mentioned that his work was considered good and that when he was working, he earned over $200 a week. During his several weeks of hospitalization, this was the one and only positive thing that he ever said about himself. This, then, is *it*! This is material that can be used in a constructive manner to help the patient to begin to make some contact with his strengths. He is already well connected with his pathology.

How much is there that can be said about cutting in a garment firm? Offhand, one certainly cannot know. But if he is willing to explore, he may very well find out a great deal about cutters and cutting. And as he begins to question his patient, let him watch the patient's face. If the patient's expression begins to brighten, or if he talks more willingly or if he seems in any way more animated, it is as though a gold mine has been struck. This may be the sole area in which the patient has derived any satisfaction. *This may be his only island of health, almost submerged in a morass of pathology* and, accordingly, almost invisible to the observer. He may continue to complain about his employer, his co-workers, his varicose veins. But this is *it*—until, in this emotionally impoverished individual, some other subject comes along. Don't turn up your nose at it.

Relief

To relieve the hospitalized patient of his extensive despair, hopelessness, and depression is to render him a most important service. During a short hospital stay, very little or no insight therapy is generally accomplished. But if the patient can be helped to "feel better"—i.e., to be less depressed, to have a sense of improved physical well-being, a slightly more optimistic outlook regarding the future—then one can say that he has been helped.

The principle underlying an approach to this goal is not obscure. Most individuals are affected (or infected) by the moods, feelings, concerns, and preoccupations of those about them. They are also affected by their own moods, feelings, concerns, and preoccupations. If, with the help of the therapist, they can concern and preoccupy themselves with nonpathology, it is more than likely that their mood and feelings will be affected in a positive way. Even if this sounds akin to "the power of positive thinking," it should not be sold short.

Deliberate attention to nonpathology interrupts a patient's morbid preoccupation with pathology. It sets him moving in a direction which may be of more value to him if the goal is to have him leave the hospital and return to some level of functioning as soon as possible. Studies done in centers all over the country indicate that the patient, when treated quickly and definitively and returned to his familiar activities, is better off than if he is removed from them for a longer period of time. Furthermore, this approach does not preclude the patient's involving himself, later on, in long-term, reconstructive treatment, if he is willing and able to do so.

In this latter respect, the first-year trainee is in no position to be of great service. He can, however, be of service in helping the patient to find something worthwhile in himself, in returning him to a position of familiarity and perhaps of some self-acceptance, and in introducing him to the possibility that longer-term psychotherapy may be of value to him.

As an example of the varied minutiae which may be seized upon to initiate the nonpathology-oriented therapeutic session, one fifty-three-year-old successful businessman came into a session speaking of a splitting headache and a feeling of mental exhaustion. When he happened to make a fleeting reference to his early life, the therapist interrupted by asking where he had lived at the time.

It turned out that his youth had been spent in a small rural community which enjoyed the vibrant changes of the seasons and the excitement of local events, shared by most of the townspeople. In describing this period of his life, which he was reluctant to do for the first few minutes, the patient's gray, tired look became less pronounced, his speech less dull, and his headache subsided. For the rest of the session he continued to speak of that time. His feeling of exhaustion and utter despair diminished considerably. Such a dramatic outcome may not be the rule, but it does demonstrate the effectiveness of bringing the patient to whatever islands of nonpathology that exist within himself.

One who can accept this method as a possible tool for helping his patient will be what might be called "open," able to recognize and to select for exploration that material which may lead to a similar outcome. This technique can be looked upon as the search for the positive, or the constructive, or the health, or, simply, the nonpathological in the patient. Admittedly, in the regressed, hopeless, schizophrenic patient, it would be most difficult to identify something of this nature. But, as in all medicine, a diagnosis that is not thought of cannot be made. Similarly, the possibility that is not believed in will not be possible.

CHAPTER II

Exploring Meanings

Goals

Beginning psychotherapists tend to leave their patients' fruitful productions too soon. In therapy, it is necessary to settle down with one theme if possible. In that way, the patient can acquire some sense of a serious interest on your part. Going rapidly from one subject to another never leads to any understanding in depth. In addition, such a technique soon leads to boredom.

It is probably accurate to say that patients enter therapy or arrive at the hospital confused, divided, and torn. All of that may or may not be clearly evident. Some come in a severely fragmented state that is obvious even to the inexperienced observer. Some psychoanalysts feel that in order to arrive at sanity, the patient must first "hit bottom." The first-year trainee, however, is not in a good position to accomplish this objective. He has neither the skill nor the necessary time with the patient. (Whether or not this is desirable is a fascinating question, but has no place in this discussion.)

One need think no less of himself if he does not use psychoanalytic techniques early in his training. There are, in fact, many other techniques he can use, especially those suited to help the patient through a sense of confusion and dividedness. It may also be argued that psychoanalytic approaches might not be helpful, in an ultimate sense, to the patient. However, one's techniques are largely influenced by one's goals.

In many psychiatric facilities, the patient is seen for a maximum of three months. What over-all objectives can be set in such a short time? Briefly, they may include any or all of the following: (1) to establish diagnosis, prognosis, and course of treatment; (2) to diminish level of anxiety and/or agitation; (3) to restore nutritional state if necessary; (4) to improve the patient's feeling about himself; (5) to reduce depression; (6) to induce a regimen of treatment with medication for continued use, if necessary; (7) to make psychotherapy available and desirable after discharge; (8) to return to a functional state; (9) to get the patient out of the hospital, preferably in an improved condition; (10) to provide the occasion for training of personnel. The order in which these goals are listed may have no particular significance. It is meant to serve only as a guide.

Content

In the psychotherapeutic session the patient may cover a wide range of subjects. This is especially true of the patient who is "productive." This usually means that he talks quite a lot. Sometimes it means that the patient says things which may lead you to feel that he is aware he is having difficulties and is making efforts to help you assist him. As the patient talks, you know that you should be alert to that special utterance which is sufficiently "significant." Then you are supposed to stop the patient with a question in order to have him elaborate. If the patient should respond to the question, he shifts the direction in which he is going and moves in the direction indicated by the therapist's question. He is often agreeable to this, and continues in the same manner as before, producing a similar quantity of material even though the core content has changed.

Depending upon the theoretical viewpoint of your supervisor, you will ask one question or another. In this way, the Freudian supervisor's student will be likely to ask questions concerning the patient's psychosexual development, etc.; the Sullivanian supervisor's student will ask questions referring to parataxic distortions, etc.; and the Horney supervisor's student will ask questions relating to idealized image, self-hatred, and so forth. (Not, of course, in all these specific terms.)

Depending upon his articulateness, sophistication, and intelligence, the patient's answers will be more or less satisfying to you. The patient will go along in almost any direction you want him to go. However revelatory that may be to you, it has little relevance to the patient's experiencing fully any particular moment of his life. Can the first-year trainee accomplish that? Is it a task for the more experienced therapist? These are questions one must answer, while searching for methods that can be used with some degree of confidence and effectiveness.

Patient Meanings

As the student reports on the therapeutic session, the supervisor may stop him and ask, "When the patient made that statement, did you ask him what he meant by it?" The reply is often "No." "Do you know what he meant?" Pause. "Well, I think I do." "What?" Pause. "Well, thus and so." "And that's what he meant?" "I can't say for sure what he meant."

This small dialogue is sufficient to illustrate that you may be conducting a therapy which is more closely related to your own thoughts and feelings than to those of your patient. This may be fruitful for you, but it is doubtful if it is of any value to the patient. Even after you have elicited the patient's meanings countless times, and can almost predict what the patient's response will be, you must repeatedly ask what is meant.

One of the basic goals of psychotherapy is to lessen the gap between the patient and his own meanings, whatever they are, through his own utterances, not the therapist's. The latter's meanings have no relevance.

The patient may, with your vigorous and enthusiastic guidance, be able to outline his psychodynamics in a short time. But what can this really mean to him? There still exists a tremendous gap between his meanings and himself. Since his meanings are himself, he continues to remain alienated from himself to the degree that he remains alienated from his meanings. The extent of this alienation is diminished as he begins to really hear what he says about the most mundane of his experiences and his thoughts.

Fact Finding

How, then, does one effectively proceed in this endeavor? Perhaps the most common opportunity for an exploration in detail arises when the patient is talking about his interactions with other persons. About his parents he says, "They never listen to me." About his wife he says, "She never wants to do what I want to do." About his child he says, "He never talks to me." You may begin to get the feeling that this person is truly ignored and isolated.

Finding your patient a pleasant, likeable person, you may feel that these people must be difficult to live with, as indeed they probably are. But a disservice can be rendered by the therapist who agrees too explicitly with his patient. To be thus reinforced in a belief that these people are impossible may only make it exceedingly difficult for the patient, if he must continue living with them.

To help make life with them easier requires that he discover his role in the family. This obvious but difficult desideratum is not an impossible objective. First, you have to find out what the "never" means. If it is really *never*, the possibility for an improved relationship would be nonexistent.

Only the patient can unfold the meaning of never. Quite often, it is revealed that the never means occasionally, frequently, or seldom. Further, the feeling of never may ensue when the patient has made some unrealistic demand, which he does not see as such. This can be uncovered only by explicit questioning in a most detailed fashion, so that the facts of the exchange are clearly outlined. The following is an example of this.

The patient complains that he and his wife cannot talk without fighting. You ask, "Every time you talk?"

Pt: "Every single time."
Th: "When was the last time?"
Pt: "Oh, I don't know."
Th: "Last week?"
Pt: "I don't remember."
Th: "Did you talk when she came to visit you Friday?"
Pt: "Sure."
Th: "Did you fight then?"
Pt: "Oh, no."
Th: "Oh, I thought you said you fought every time you talked."
Pt: "Well, not every time."
Th: "I thought you said every time."
Pt: "Well, no."
Th: "Did you fight when she came on Tuesday?"
Pt: "I don't think so. But this is different. In the hospital we don't fight."
Th: "Why not?"
Pt: "It's different."
Th: "How different?"
Pt: (smiling) "We're on our good behavior."
Th: "How?"
Pt: "More polite."
Th: "How, more polite?"

Details

The patient is then encouraged to describe precisely what he means by polite, and how this effort keeps them from fighting. In trying to clarify this point, ostensibly for your benefit, the patient is making contact with himself. If he can make this connection, you will note that it is made through a constructive reference on his part (politeness) rather than through reference to pathology.

By this reference to a more acceptable means of relating to his wife, the patient has the opportunity to discover that there is another way to be with her. He may not be interested in such a possibility, and it may even make him more anxious. But this is a risk you may take, if your patient is ever to move away from his compulsive patterns which dictate the quality of his relationships.

It may even occur to him that the fighting is not just an unavoidable visitation from outer space, or caused by a "bitchy" wife, but that it is brought about by a state of mutual rudeness. While this realization does not change the dynamics of the mutual, unconscious demands each probably makes upon the other, it may serve to drive a tiny wedge into the patient's tightly constructed defense system with which he maintains his image of himself as the wronged, and of his wife as the wrong-doer. This is referred to by Ronald Laing (*Knots,* 1970) when he speaks of the "baddies" and the "goodies." The patient here is the goody and the wife is the baddy. Of course, she regards him as the baddy and herself as the goody. From their respective positions each is completely accurate in the assessment of the other.

This kind of exploration does not require you or your patient to delve into psychodynamic formulations which the patient may have no interest in and with which you have not had sufficient experience. Such a direct, fact-finding approach, conducted gently and never in the spirit of criticism, not only uncovers important data, but gives both you and your patient a sense of knowing what is going on. Further, it may give you a sense of security in conducting the therapy.

More Details

The approach requires a good deal of patience and perseverance on your part. This is so because initially the patient usually cannot describe any minute vignette in a detailed manner. He cannot even think of an example when the therapist asks him to be specific regarding some generalization. Many psychiatric patients could go through long-term treatment making only generalizations. It is the therapist's task to help the patient be specific.

Even after he has described a particular episode to illustrate his feeling, the patient is willing to let it go at that. The patient's part in the episode must be ascertained, however—exactly what was said, how it was said (tone, pitch, etc.), the expression on his face (described as well as he can), how he felt when he was saying what. All of this takes a good deal of time, and may often use the greater part of the therapeutic session.

You may often fail to get the response you are seeking. But it is worthwhile to keep persisting. It is also necessary to mention that the supervisor is in a position to sense when you are going too far with this technique, if you do not. When you recognize that the patient can no longer stay with you, you may stop your exploration and permit the patient to wander as he will (free associate, if need be). This does not mean that the technique being described is discarded. It is put aside for the time, to be picked up again when indicated.

Here and Now

This technique has therapeutic value, but not because of the possible accuracy of the reporting. There may still be extensive distortion. Its value is that the patient must attend to himself in a way he has never before experienced. He must struggle to remember words, thoughts, feelings which are all aspects of himself.

These are not the thoughts and feelings about something that happened twenty years ago, or even one year ago. They are those of last night when he went to the drugstore to get toothpaste, and today in the lunchroom. This is life *now*, as he is presently experiencing it, good, bad, or indifferent. This is the only life he can make contact with, or that has any immediate meaning to him. This is the life that coincides with his illness now, his anxiety, his fears, etc.

At this point, he may find it difficult to feel any contact with a dead parent, or a married sibling, or some event in his past life. Yes, he can talk *about* them, but sometimes no connection takes place. If talking *about* events becomes only an intellectual exercise, its value to the patient will be quite limited.

There is a certain simplicity about the kind of questioning and picayune involvement necessary to engage the patient in this exploration; yet this technique is often more difficult than one might suppose. The supervisor will find that he must refer to it over and over again, citing frequent samples. Sometimes you will feel that this line of questioning is a lot of nonsense, and that it doesn't get to the "bottom" of things. You may, therefore, be resistant to using it. It's difficult to appreciate its value, until it has actually been tried. Then you can note the quality of the patient's involvement, and how the many distortions which have been elaborated are made evident.

The patient distorts as a defense. The therapist distorts largely on the basis of his preconceptions, which are best dealt with by the supervisor. The latter helps to explode them, if necessary, by guiding the supervisee to elicit the patient's explication of his position at any given moment.

If You Can't Swim . . . .

An attempt to engage the patient in a dialogue regarding his feelings about the therapist may be much too threatening for both patient and therapist, and is hardly relevant and certainly not necessary at this tender stage. After all, what can you say, having asked the patient how he feels about you, when the patient replies that he does not feel that you are sufficiently experienced, or that you do not seem to understand him, etc.?

These observations may undoubtedly be true; and you

need not defend yourself on that score. But it is the rare young trainee who does not feel some chagrin when told how incompetent he is. This feeling can significantly interfere with his belief that, despite his inexperience, he can be of some help to his patients. In some instances, he can be of great help, but not because of his fund of information and therapeutic skills. Unless he is emotionally equipped to hear the bald truth and is able to use it in a constructive manner to further his understanding of the patient, as well as himself as a therapist, there is no point in placing himself in this position.

Please remember that we are talking about beginning psychotherapists here. Therefore, such an approach might be indicated after you have acquired the experience sufficient to know when to use such an approach, and your goals when you use it. The inexperienced worker has other alternatives. In time, he will gain not only the experience but the necessary confidence he needs with his patient. Neither he nor the supervisor can be too ambitious in the early months.

Distortions

You need first to know how exaggerated the responses of the patient may be to the most trivial of events. With some patients, you learn that there is no particular order of importance regarding their experiences. Everything is a "big deal" for the patient. This is what is meant by a patient's sensitivity. The concept of sensitivity becomes less of a vague term which may be used to describe any patient. It becomes an understanding of the extreme guardedness and suspiciousness of each patient.

The patient may be "sensitive" to the way an attendant places the cup on the table at dinner. If the handle is placed toward him, the patient feels that he can trust the attendant. If the handle is turned away from him, the assumption may be made that the attendant is saying that he does not like him and is out to "get him." This is one of the minutiae that you will find out about. Only the patient can describe this, but he will not, unless you find the way to bring him to do it.

I do not refer here to the delusional patient who has worked this out in a complicated but clearly apparent system, but rather to the garden-variety patient, who may have this thought in a fleeting fantasy. If questioned, he often cannot remember such an occurrence, because his attention was quickly deflected by another equally threatening experience requiring, in turn, his entire attention. The psychiatric patient may feel exhausted at times because of the tension required to maintain this level of attentiveness. He is constantly being distracted from communications with others about him and from their show of interest and, perhaps, concern for him. He is much too preoccupied with this or that fantasy to be concerned with others' moves toward him and with his own possible feelings in response to their overtures.

Who Said What?

Perhaps the best way to educate the novice to this approach is by employing it with him. The facts of his report of the therapeutic session cannot be taken at face value without questioning them. The supervisor has to ask what this means and what that means. This does not refer to latent meanings in what the patient says. It is much too early to confuse the problem with this kind of convoluted thinking.

The goal here is to find out what the patient's meanings are, not the foggy interpretations of the trainee. Did the patient use a particular word or is it the therapist's word? Exactly what was the patient's terminology? Was it clear or was an assumption being made about what the patient was saying? If it was an assumption, what does the assumption mean?

Does the therapist know that an assumption is his own guess, which may or may not be accurate? Does he know that the accuracy of the assumption can be confirmed only by the patient himself? The therapist needs to know this unequivocally. This does not mean to say that he may not act upon an unconfirmed assumption, if he feels that it serves a therapeutic function.

The matter of assumptions and preconceptions is in the realm of the psychotherapist's fantasy. In confronting the patient, he has the task of constantly eliminating his preconceptions, as information is supplied by the patient. Unless this is done, it is possible that he will begin to see his preconceptions as the patient's data. And, unless he is carefully questioned about this, he may remain quite unaware of this switch. He might continue to assume that he hears and understands all that the patient is telling him, an assumption which may be some distance from the truth.

Questions

There are differences in the approach to a first-year trainee and what is suitable with the more experienced one. It is perhaps difficult for the experienced supervisor to keep in mind the naiveté and ignorance of his students.

Unfortunately, the student often does the same thing with the supervisor that he does with the patient. He assumes that he understands what the supervisor is saying and therefore does not question him in depth as to the real meanings and usefulness of what he is being taught. He may not even know enough to say, "What you are saying does not seem to fit in with my thinking. Can you explain that in another way, or give me an example of what you mean?"

Or, as is so often the case, he will not question at all, because of a sense of shame, feeling (as is the bane of so many professional people) that he must know it all—even before it is possible to do so! So he nods wisely and silently, giving the impression that he is absorbing everything, and will use it all in the next session with the patient. Thus, the supervisor must beware of the silent trainee who has no questions.

It is his task to help the trainee to find these questions, so that he can, finally, learn that ignorance lying in the path of understanding has to be wrestled with, not discarded, overlooked, or met with shame. Only through a recognition of our ignorance can we be motivated to learn. Surely, it follows that if one does not know that one does not know, how can one be interested in learning something that one does not know one does not know!

CHAPTER III

Assumptions and Preconceptions

Definition

Much of the work done in psychotherapy and psychoanalysis rests upon a base of assumptions and preconceptions. To the extent that the therapist is conscientious and self-searching, he will constantly examine these assumptions and preconceptions.

However, before we assume that we understand what is meant by these terms, let us define them according to their most common usage. To *assume* is to take something for granted, or to suppose that something is true without proof or confirmation that it is. Proof is a difficult concept, not to be bandied about in psychiatry. Confirmation is a gentler term with which one can work effectively.

For our purpose, the definition of assumption is: that which is accepted by the psychotherapist to be so, with or without evidence, before it has been *confirmed* by the patient. The key word is *confirmation*. At that point, where the patient makes a statement validating the therapist's assumption, it becomes a fact and is no longer an assumption.

Use of Assumptions

There is no attempt here to decry use of assumptions in psychotherapeutic work. It would be difficult indeed to practice without them. Great reliance upon assumptions by some therapists, however, may result more from the nature of the therapist than from necessity for such reliance.

Furthermore, I am not at all certain that effective therapy could not take place with the making of minimal assumptions or possibly none at all. But this tempting digression must be resisted.

Assumptions are made most often in the area of trying to understand the patient's meanings. A patient with a severe block about working was talking about "making efforts." The therapist asked, "How do you feel about making efforts?"—assuming that he already understood how the patient felt about this. (The therapist himself had a positive view regarding effort, having learned early in life that efforts bring rewards of one kind or another, and that one feels good making an effort and accomplishing something. But he had been advised to ask this kind of question and he did.)

Making the assumption that he knew how the patient felt, the therapist's rationale in asking this question was that he wanted the patient to become more involved in his own experiences of effort. The latter replied that, for him, effort meant drudgery, exhaustion, disgust, resentment, rage and guilt. (This did not come out in one sentence.) In view of his assumption, the therapist was surprised at uncovering all those feelings. His surprise kept him more silent than usual, inadvertently giving the patient an opportunity to elaborate further.

Confirmation

While many of the therapist's assumptions may be correct in the sense that they are often confirmed by the patient, it must always be kept in mind that they do not become *data* until such confirmation. Even when there seems to be unequivocal evidence for an assumption, it is still an assumption until the patient confirms it. I am reiterating that much of our work is done on the basis of assumption, and, as stated earlier, this is the nature of the work. My concern is only that one be aware of this state of affairs.

The patient referred to above went on to relate how, as a

teenager, he had to help his mother with her housekeeping. She apparently gave him the jobs she herself disliked. He was obliged to clean the toilet, polish the brass plumbing, and perform other such tasks. She was a perfectionist; the brass had to shine, and the toilet had to smell clean.

At this point the following assumptions might possibly have been made: (1) that the patient hated not only this work, but that he would hate all subsequent work of this nature, or perhaps any other kind; (2) that he would be furious with his mother; (3) that he would feel guilty for being so angry with her and for being so "lazy"; (4) that this work was an insult to his masculinity and an indignity to him as a human being. These are all assumptions.

Let us see how many of them the patient subsequently confirmed. He revealed that he could make the necessary efforts and could satisfy her (which was something). But in doing so, he developed an antipathy for all such work and a rage against his mother for "forcing" him to submit to such an indignity. The sense of guilt was not confirmed at that time. While it was probably present, that had to remain in the realm of assumption rather than fact. What he did say was that all of these feelings, as he became aware of them, had apparently infected him with a distaste for the thought of making efforts of any kind, not merely with respect to toilets, brass fittings, and demanding mothers.

Obviously, a lecture (which some trainees find themselves giving) on the merits of making efforts would not get very far with this patient. Nor is he going to immediately form a new view on making efforts. However, if he has had the opportunity to hear himself describe his feelings on the matter, this might serve as a minute scratch on the surface, a possible starting point in a future consideration of his development. He might even be able to say to himself, "No wonder I hate to work at anything," still without being able to work after he has said it.

It is also possible, however, that the patient may feel some slight relief. For remember that the therapist has assumed that the patient felt guilt. If this assumption is correct, there might very well follow a sense of relief. The assumption of guilt is a reasonable one to make, for is not the making of effort in the great American tradition—as well as loving one's mother, regardless? If the patient could not make these efforts, then one might assume that he felt pretty much as one of the "boys" and not "one of the men." While many patients may not be able to provide this kind of material, the principle of validating one's assumptions remains.

Unpredictable

An assumption differs from a preconception in that the therapist may not be able to tell anyone what assumption he will make as he works with his patient. They keep coming up as the work proceeds. One assumption after another can be made in that the therapist will think that he knows what the patient means in everything he says, as long as his speech seems logical.

With illogical patients, or with the patients who use neologisms or word salads, one proceeds more carefully, because of a realization that he does not understand what his patient is saying. With such a patient, one may become impatient and find it difficult to work; but one will not make the mistake of thinking that he understands what the patient is saying.

There is the likelihood that no assumptions can be made with such a patient. Unless the therapist has had an experience akin to that of the patient's and has used similar terms, or has already tried to treat such a patient, he can have no basis for making assumptions. They can be made only when he feels he has something in common with the patient and can believe that the patient means what the therapist thinks the patient is meaning.

Preconception as Prejudice

Preconceptions do not have the quality of immediacy that assumptions do. They may be defined as opinions previously formed, and believed to apply to a patient even before the therapist ever sees the patient. In this regard, a preconception has the same characteristics as a prejudice. The particular set of preconceptions the trainee has depends upon the books he has read, the theory he has studied, the position of his supervisor and so forth.

The novice usually has some background before he starts to work with his patients. But sometimes the less he knows about theoretical formulations, and the fewer preconceptions he has when he encounters his first patients, the more open he will be to his patients' productions.

One-Way Bias

It is not uncommon to hear a patient unfold dynamic material. Of course, he does not label it as such. It is for the supervisor to make such an identification if the significance of the material has not been recognized. To the extent that one can remain free of prejudice, or preconception, he will also remain free to listen to the patient unfold his *strengths* as well as his pathology.

While many preconceptions are held about the patient's pathology, few are held about the patient's health. In other words, you may be biased regarding the patient's illness, but not his state of health. This might seem like a good thing. But your preconceptions regarding the patient's pathology stand in the way of gaining (1) a clear view of the *raison d'être* of the patient's defenses (pathology), and (2) a clear view of the existence and development of the patient's actual resources, which are always present in some degree. If the patient is seen only from a preconceived point of view of pathology, *very small islands of health* that every patient has within the sea of what appears an overwhelming morass of illness may well be missed.

Diagnosis

The novice eagerly ferrets out all the evidence he needs to

make his diagnosis and to defend it. This is a requirement he must fulfill for many reasons. But the making of a diagnosis, *per se*, in no way helps the patient. If he is helped, it is inadvertent, and results from his feeling that there is a person who has some concern for his welfare. There is no gainsaying this, as long as the therapist knows that in collecting data for a diagnosis, this is his primary intention.

Benevolent Curiosity

The therapist who is impelled by a *benevolent curiosity* when he is with his patient will be less likely to rest with assumptions and preconceptions. He will want to put assumptions to the test and find out whether or not they can be confirmed. He will discover that each patient unwittingly evolves his own theory of illness, if given the opportunity to do so. Once the curious therapist makes this discovery, he can truly be a Columbus with each one of his patients and learn that there are basic similarities, as well as differences, in all patients. In this way, learning is rooted in one's own experience with each patient, rather than in hearsay. Then the trainee will learn how to avoid orthodoxies when they are of little service to him.

CHAPTER IV
Use of Assumptions

The Silent Patient

What can I do if the patient won't talk to me and I know nothing about him? How can I help him? Implicit in these questions are three goals: (1) to get the patient to talk; (2) to find out something about the patient; (3) to help him.

Instead of pursuing his work, the trainee may just wallow in feelings of helplessness and inadequacy. Since anger is often first cousin to helplessness, he may also feel frustrated in his attempts and a little angry with both the patient and himself for his incompetence. Other people get patients to talk—why can't he? He may have this thought even though he has other patients who talk with him and whom he can supposedly help. Isn't therapy, after all, inextricably bound up with the patient's verbalizing? Isn't it?

Nonetheless, this therapist has much with which to comfort himself. His second goal—to find out something about the patient—has already been fulfilled, for he can assume that he knows a good deal about the patient. There is no magic or clairvoyance here; most patients share certain basic feelings. While their obvious symptomatology may vary considerably and each one's verbalizations be unique, most patients share several characteristics in common. More important, however, is that these features are accepted only as assumptions, until confirmatory data is obtained from the patient.

When you proceed on the basis of these assumptions, you can feel that you have a great deal of information about the patient. You might then feel less frustrated and angry, and be able to get down to the business of attending to the patient. Negative feelings can only interfere with efficacy. Believing that you have information about the patient makes it easier for you to get the patient to find something to say.

First, you can rest assured that the patient is not deliberately trying to frustrate you. The patient may be too depressed to have anything to say. He may be so hopeless that he feels no one can help him. He may be so suspicious that he can trust no one. Whatever his motive for being uncommunicative, it is an old pattern of behavior that follows him, not a sudden attack of wishing-to-frustrate-the-therapist. In almost every case, it has nothing to do with the person of the therapist, who only burdens himself needlessly if he thinks *he* is at fault. I say in *almost* every case in order to account for the occasional therapist whose manner is offensive, or who is truly so inept that he indeed turns the patient off, and whose rapport with the patient can be measured only in the negative range on an appropriate scalometer. Surprisingly enough, few therapists turn patients off to this degree. This is because they are, across the board, a dedicated group, and because most patients are generally cooperative. These two factors are significant in achieving a working rapport in early encounters.

Patient Anxiety

What can you assume you know about the patient? First, you can safely assume that your patient is anxious. Sometimes, but not always, in writing their reports, psychotherapists state that the patient is quite anxious. I would amend that by saying that *all* patients are anxious. Anxiety may be more apparent in some than in others. But to assume that some patients are not anxious would be inaccurate and, therefore, a disservice to the patient. It would also distort the therapist's approach.

Ranges of mild, moderate, and severe may be applied to anxiety as to any other symptom. When the therapist describes his patient as quite anxious, he usually means severely anxious. The inexperienced therapist may find it difficult to spot mild anxiety. But please assume that it's there, because it is and probably more than mild. This is especially true of the hospitalized patient. Remember, he doesn't enter the hospital because of a little disturbance. He comes in heavily loaded with difficulties with which he can no longer cope. A little disturbance could have been handled outside of the hospital. Even when he seems tranquil and content, the hospitalized patient is like an iceberg; there's a great deal more pathology beneath the surface than meets the eye.

Assume, then, that your patient is probably experiencing a great deal of anxiety. What can be done with this knowledge? The third goal, to help the patient, now becomes pressing. Since anxiety is often such a nonspecific symptom and so difficult for a patient to describe, especially when he is not fully aware of it, how specific can treatment for anxiety be? Certain drugs can be specific and each therapist has the obligation to see to it that the patient receives well-supervised drug treatment if it is indicated. But what can you do personally to help your patient, especially when severe anxiety in the patient is often anxiety-provoking for the therapist?

Therapist Anxiety

While the patient does not realize how anxious you may be feeling, he can sense your anxiety when it reaches certain proportions. He may not be fully aware, but he somehow gets the message. This is a disquieting condition for the patient, for your anxiety tells him that his position is indeed a precarious one. The patient wants to feel less anxious, but he reasons that if his therapist is also feeling anxious there must be something frightening and overwhelming going on. So the direct-proportion formula is applicable here: to the extent that the therapist is anxious, to that extent will he be unable to be of service to his patient.

This implies that you can do your best regarding the alleviation of your patient's anxiety by being minimally anxious yourself. This is one of the most effective techniques for coping with exorbitant anxiety in some patients. But how is this accomplished, especially when *you* are anxious? You might be comforted by knowing that many of your fellow workers also become anxious when confronting a very anxious patient. After you have rid yourself of the problem of feeling uniquely incompetent because of fears, you are better prepared to examine certain facts.

Old Anxiety

The psychiatric patient has been anxious for a long time. While there may have been an acute resurgence of anxiety, which led to his seeking treatment, anxiety is something that the patient is familiar with and with which he has learned to live. Although his defenses may not be working well, he does have them; as soon as a little pressure is relieved, he will be able to make his defenses operative once again. With all due respect to the patient's suffering, the therapist may nevertheless be more impressed by the patient's suffering than the patient is.

It is comforting, in a sense, to know that the patient is familiar with his anxiety; although it causes him suffering, he can tolerate it better than the therapist imagines he can. This is something inexperienced workers do not know. In fact, the sudden absence of all anxiety (if it were possible) is something that might cause a patient to become disoriented and fall apart. He might not know himself without his mantle, and he might become confused by this new person (feeling) he feels himself to be.

Safety

Mentioned above was the relief of pressure. It is important that you know what pressures exist and how they may be relieved. Initially, most hospitalized patients are frightened and concerned with their immediate physical and psychic welfare. To feel incapable of caring for oneself or one's family causes great pain. Within hours, the newly hospitalized patient's position shifts from an impotent, anguished concern to an awareness of having every need cared for. He now has the choice of no longer taking any responsibility for himself in any way, or of exercising responsibility for himself to some degree. The latter, of course, depends upon his state, and upon the particular psychiatric facility. Such a shift brings with it some relief of tension and anxiety.

The patient further feels that he is safe or, at least, safer than he was before hospitalization. Both trainee and patient can take comfort in the fact that there is experienced professional or paraprofessional personnel available for the care of the patient and that they are neither flustered nor made anxious when a new patient is hospitalized. The novice does well to take cues from the permanent hospital staff, for he will not only learn from them, but he might also be influenced by their tension-free attitudes and quiet authority. You would also do well to appreciate the fact that most patients are not aware of the problem you are having with your own uncertainties, self-doubts, and general ineptitude.

The Therapist is Not All

You need to know that the course of the patient's progress does not rest solely upon your therapeutic acumen. Such knowledge may relieve anxiety regarding treatment of the patient. At this stage, the most effective tool you possess is a relatively anxiety-free outlook. The patient wants to be reassured that he is not in such a bad way, after all. Words are often not necessary here. More important, if the patient senses that you are not "up-tight" about his condition, he is more reassured by this than anything you can say or do. To repeat, the therapist who realizes that there are many therapeutic forces at play besides his own will be comforted that his own obligation is not as critical as he may have felt it to be and will, as a consequence, feel less anxious.

A situation illustrating the effectiveness of the anxiety-free therapist occurred when a young psychiatrist, in office practice for about one year, was treating one of his patients who had come in with a severe, acute anxiety attack. Within ten minutes the doctor realized that his own response would preclude his helping the patient. He excused himself and called on an experienced colleague who shared the suite with him. Fortunately, his colleague was free for the hour and came in and sat with the patient. He said little beyond introducing himself and asking if he could help. He offered no explanation for his being there. The patient gradually quieted down, and at the end of the hour thanked the doctor, saying, "I'll be alright now," and left. Such drama may not be common, but it illustrates the impact of the tension-free psychotherapist.

Depression

Seldom does it occur that the patient who becomes hospitalized is also not depressed. Even the manic patient has his substructure of deep depression. Thus, the therapist can make the assumption that his patient is depressed as well as anxious. If this is so, hypothetically, you know a great deal more about the patient than the patient has told you or may ever be able to tell you.

In order to acquire such hypothetical knowledge, the therapist has to be familiar with certain basics, common to most depressions. Depression may be characterized by the following: (1) A sense of irrevocable loss. There may be a real loss of a job, a spouse, etc., but more often the loss is largely experienced as loss of status, aspiration, competence, etc., whereas no real change has actually taken place. (2) A feeling of helplessness, and guilt for being so helpless and therefore a burden to one's family. This is where one often hears the phrase, "They'd all be better off if I were dead." That is usually accompanied by floods of tears. (3) A pervasive rage, which is inner-directed and provides the rationale for the clinical manifestations of depression. While there may be towering rage directed at some family member, the patient cannot reconcile this feeling with his image of himself, nor can he tolerate the murderous possibilities of the expression of such rage. He must thus press down, or *de*-press, other feelings as well. This is manifest when the patient states he has no interest in anything; he can't be amused, or pleased, feel joy or affection towards his children. He somehow manages to *de*-press his physiology also. He feels tired—tired! He feels heavy. He has no appetite, can't sleep. He doesn't want to move, and so forth. In long-term severe depression, it is not inconceivable that his blood chemistry may undergo changes as well. All of this obviously takes him out of the running. If he can maintain that state, his anger cannot be threatening to anyone. When he is safely hospitalized, the patient can be helped to experience his anger in small doses and begin to direct it toward one or another. The consummate skill required of the therapist at this point is discussed elsewhere. Suffice it to say that, depending upon how it is handled, this move can be both relieving and constructive. On occasion, it may be irrevocably destructive in terms of shattered relationships. (4) A feeling of overwhelming hopelessness. The depressed patient's final "coup" is to decide that any change from his present state is impossible. This accounts for the deep hopelessness in depressed patients. This is one of the stickiest aspects with which the therapist has to deal. Of all the characteristics of depression, abject hopelessness is perhaps the most infectious. Few therapists who work in hospitals are not infected by it at one time or another. When they are not, it is a blessing. Freedom from this affliction makes it more tolerable for you to be with your patient and to retain a sense of optimism. (5) An abyss of self-hatred. It is difficult to separate the kind of rage described above from the patient's feeling of self-hatred. Rage is often associated with a particular person or situation. It is something almost pulsatingly tangible and can be easily associated with something definite. Self-hatred on the other hand is a pervasive, invasive, insidious, extensive, corrosive, all-encompassing feeling that may have a nebulous, unreachable quality, making it difficult to deal with at any particular moment. This is not to say that one has to treat this feeling in the hospitalized psychiatric patient. Remember, we are discussing some of the dynamics of patient behavior with which you have to be familiar, but not necessarily talk about with the patient.

Open Questions

An awareness of the existence of these forces in the patient gives you much information about him. Such information can make you feel more comfortable and secure; it makes it easier for you to talk with the patient, who is not really such a mystery, even though the latter does not volunteer much information. Armed with this knowledge, you can now ask of your recalcitrant patient, "Have you felt recently that you sustained the loss of something precious to you?" This is, of course, a walloping question. But if it is asked gently and followed by a silence giving the patient a chance to consider it, there is a good likelihood that he will make some answer. He may also start to cry, or even wail. You might do well to remember that a good cry is good medicine. You should allow the patient to have his cry (for not too long) and then ask, "Can you tell me what you're crying about?" You may think you know what the patient is crying about, but that won't do the patient any good. If you put words into the patient's mouth—"Aren't you crying about this or that?" or "Are you crying because you're so angry?"—the patient might very well say yes. And where does one go from there?

The more open the question, the more can be elicited from the patient. Once a good working relationship is established, the content of the questions may become more specific. In the initial, relieving phase of treatment, the patient's talking about anything and your attentive listening are usually adequate to achieve the goal of partial relief. In psychotherapy, however, the cure is not merely talking. It is talking about the elements that are central to the evolution of the patient's strength as well as his illness. The patient does not offer this material himself. The therapist elicits with appropriate questions. He may then learn what is necessary to help his patient toward mental health.

CHAPTER V
Notes on Depression

Every Patient is Depressed

Depression is a ball game unto itself. Both as to diagnosis and treatment, it is one of the most difficult clinical entities. Although severe depression can be diagnosed today by laymen, mild or moderate depression may very well be missed by the inexperienced professional worker. Furthermore, one should not be lulled into a sense of security by the adjective "mild." A depression is a serious clinical entity, whether it is rated severe or not.

Other more obvious symptoms—agitation, anxiety, or somatic complaints—may obscure the depression and lead the therapist to attempt to attend these primarily. While these symptoms may have a dramatic quality, an underlying mild depression may have limited your patient for most of his life. Because it is my belief that every psychiatric patient comes into treatment with some measure of depression, the treatment program should include, at least, recognition of the existing depression and some attempt to deal with it.

Feelings of Incompetence

Included among the many components usually present in depression, especially the severe one, are feelings of incompetence, inadequacy, and worthlessness. The patient fully believes he is "low man" and will argue relentlessly, "You just don't know how little I really know about that.'' A severely depressed patient once insisted that, although he had graduated from a dental school, had been licensed, and had practiced and supported a family for many years, he knew nothing about his work.

To argue against this position is usually fruitless. One reason is because there is often some grounding, however slight, for such statements. While it was true that the patient's term ''nothing'' was a gross exaggeration, it was also true that there were large areas of dentistry with which he was no longer familiar. He had been treating youngsters for the most part and had referred complications to a specialist. It was conceivable that, over the years, he would feel less and less competent in many areas of his profession where his only exposure had been during his early training.

Clues to Check

Taking any exaggerations into consideration, it is well to listen carefully and to believe, judiciously, what the patient says about himself. However alienated he may be, the patient is still the best source of information about himself. His view of others may be open to some question, but he needs to feel that someone believes him when he talks about himself. You can spare yourself a sense of hopelessness if you remember three points: (1) the patient may be speaking a somewhat exaggerated truth when he derogates himself and deplores his ignorance; (2) he may be indeed ignorant about the areas of his work, but there is good reason for this when his work is limited to a small segment of his field and he has not bothered to keep informed in a broad sense; and (3) he is not telling you about the things he does know and can do.

Among his assets, in this case, may be the kind of personality which puts children at their ease immediately. He may be able to proceed with a routine examination and make it something of a fun experience for the child. This particular incompetent (in his view) dentist may have a talent for alleviating anxiety or even avoiding the arousal of anxiety. He may have a particularly gentle touch, which is a precious gift in professionals who must, upon occasion, inflict physical pain.

Let the Patient Tell

I think the point has been sufficiently made that while the patient is bemoaning his limitations, he is not informing you as to his capabilities and his formerly demonstrated talents. He is not in touch with these (alienated from) during a period of depression, but one can assume that there are strengths, and be assured that this patient is not the epitome of pathology that he believes himself to be.

Such an assumption leads to the use of techniques I have described earlier. If you assume the existence of assets in a depressed patient, you are alert to whatever clue is presented regarding the positive side of the clinical picture. The smallest hint has to be seized with avidity. This patient may say in a self-deprecating manner, "I can only treat children." The clue here lies in the words—"can treat." The word "only" is the self-effacing part of the statement. "Oh," replies the therapist, following the clue, "are they difficult patients to treat?" "Not really," says the patient sadly. "That's the only reason I can treat them." ZONG! Again the double play—"can treat" and "only." He's still giving himself the business. Pause. Give the patient a chance to say something else. If he does not, there's always time for another question. If he starts with how afraid he is to treat adults, you wait for an opening and then come in, still following the clue, "I would have thought children would be difficult. Don't they cry and squirm about a lot?"

"They rarely do with me," the patient says, sighing.

"How come?"

"Unless it's a real emergency, I never treat them the first time they come." (Period! The patient is not going to give you anything for nothing.)

"What do you do then?"

"Well, I have a kind of little routine." (Pause.)
"What is it?"

Some workers may view this behavior as a sadistic attempt on the part of the patient to frustrate the therapist. That may be. But it's more encouraging for you to believe that the patient just can't whip up enough interest yet to participate in this exchange. If you persist, you may eventually elicit the information that the dentist's assistant is ready with some plaster of paris for each child. Little rubber forms of Snoopy and other Peanuts characters permit each child to become an instant sculptor and artist. For while his creation is drying, the child is permitted to paint another one that is already dry. He may then take this home with him for his mother to keep forever and ever. Can you imagine how he may rush to see the dentist the next time?

Information of this nature does not come out unless it is painstakingly elicited. When it comes out at all, it can be therapeutic. The patient, who has been wallowing in an abyss of self-reproach, guilt, and self-hatred, has emerged briefly from that abyss in telling about his technique for the avoidance of anxiety in his little patients. Somewhere, even in his present state of depression and despair, he is proud of his technique and has a good feeling about it.

It is possible that this man has not had an opportunity to think of himself in such terms for months. Remember that the severely ill patient often has a history of at least weeks or months of severe symptomatology. No one has been able to get him to speak of himself in positive terms. Don't think that no one has tried. Many well-meaning friends have said, in effect, "But look how your patients love you!" "Look how successful you've been!" "Look at the nice family you've raised!" He will have arguments for all of them.

In pursuing a clue, the therapist is not telling the patient anything. The patient is telling the therapist. This is what makes the difference. But he's not telling anything voluntarily. Nor would he have expressed anything if he had not been asked specific questions after he gave only a tiny clue. Following an exposure of a strength, the therapist need not state, "You see, you're not such a bad dentist after all," because the patient will rush to contradict and insist that he is indeed a failure. In so doing, he quickly loses the after-effect of his previous productions. It is sometimes a good idea to terminate the session at that point, so that the patient can mull over what he had inadvertently revealed to himself as well as to the therapist.

Not having made obvious summarizing remarks at the end of the session, you have not distracted the patient from what he was saying. He has no need to defend himself from the pressure of your optimism. You have, with your small questions, made him examine, come closer to what he values in himself, even if only for a few moments. You need never tell him this. Getting him to do it is the therapeutic element, not telling him that he has done it.

Many inexperienced therapists have a great need to tell their patients, in one way or another, what they (patient or therapist) are doing while doing it. Such objectivity has no place here, for it may invest the therapeutic situation with an artificiality for which the patient has little use, as he already is greatly lacking in spontaneous responses. Such clinical observations are best reserved for the supervisory hour. No patient should be burdened with a gratuitous opinion of his progress, or with your self-congratulatory need to keep him thus informed.

Join Them

Some severely depressed patients give no clues whatsoever. Or at least it would seem so. If this is true, then the technique described above cannot be put to use. If you feel that the patient can and will talk of nothing but how stupid, inadequate, and depressed he is, then the *join-them* technique may be useful. Therapeutically, there are two possible immediate effects: (1) the patient will feel that he has finally found a sympathetic ear and will continue to relate to you, and (2) the patient will feel that you understand him, while all those others were always telling him what to do and how much he could do before he fell ill. In terms of establishing a working relationship in a difficult situation, one could ask for no better response from the nonresponsive, depressed patient.

First Move

The first move of the join-them technique is an implicit agreement with the patient's position. One must be very careful about explicit statements here, because the patient can use them later here to crucify both the therapist and himself. The join-them technique has at its center an acceptance of the patient as he presents himself. The patient can identify that acceptance almost without question. Your attitude, your questions, your entire approach communicates: "Yes, I see that you are terribly depressed. You feel rotten, unhappy, alone and abandoned. You do seem to be limited in the areas that you say you are."

The patient is being given nothing to buck. He does not have to keep convincing anyone, and incidentally himself, how sick he is. You already know it. He knows it. You know that he knows you know it. Some therapists do not realize that their approach leads certain patients to feel that they have to keep fighting the therapist to make their positions clear. To the extent that the patient has to impress you with his weaknesses (pathology), he is distracted from the more important and essential work of discovering his strengths.

One danger of the join-them technique is an exaggerated and therefore inappropriate enthusiasm. While you are accepting the pathology and allying yourself with the patient, you do not need to give the impression that you are cheering for the patient's pathology. Psychopathology is a tragic, deplorable finding, and one must never lose sight of that fact.

Respect for this finding is not the equivalent of approval or condonation. There is a distinction to be made here, of which the young worker may be unaware. Although the surgeon must respect every aspect of his patient's broken leg, he certainly does not need to approve of it or to condone its existence in order to treat it effectively.

The inexperienced worker, in his zeal to establish "good rapport" with the patient, often falls into the trap of regarding pathology in such a way as to cause the patient to invest it with further complicated feelings. These may ultimately make it more difficult for him to be helped to move away from it.

Low Key

A clear, sympathetic, but dispassionate acceptance of the patient's pathology helps him to put it in proper context. It exists. It is a handicap. The patient wants relief. You will help him to obtain relief. You and he will work together on this. Patients are often unsure of the reason for their hospitalization; they are unsure of even the most superficial aspects of their pathology; they are therefore unsure of their part or the therapist's part in the entire therapeutic endeavor.

Second Move

After the points of the first move are clear, the therapist may make his second move. The timing of these moves is as significant in this process as the moves themselves. The second move concerns the patient's intentions regarding his pathology. We know what the therapist's intentions are; we need not belabor that point. But both therapist and patient had better find out what the patient intends to do, if anything, about this pathology. In most cases, I'm sorry to say, the patient intends to do nothing. All he wants is relief, which is understandable. However, when the relief has been secured to some degree, a desired psychotherapeutic effect must be attempted.

Rather than tell the patient that he must now try to rid himself of enough of his pathology so that he can function again, one might ask a question like, "Are you interested in doing anything about your depression?" While it may seem that the only obvious answer from a rational patient would be, "I want to be rid of it," he may not be able to actually articulate these words. If he can hear himself saying them, he places himself in the best position to assure his being helped. He must indeed "want to be rid of it," or you can be certain he'll keep it.

The critical words, "I want to be rid of it," remain difficult for the patient where unconscious motivations drive him to maintain the depression. If you are patient, he may begin to experience a niggle of resistance against stating such an obvious fact—of course, anyone would want to be rid of an incapacitating depression!

If the patient cannot come up with it, you may ask about the ways in which the patient feels he can live *with* his depression. An answer to this would require the patient's considering the ways he might diminish, but not give up, the devastating effects of his depression. If he must keep it, yet not feel that you would snatch it from him, he might be able to cooperate in finding ways to live with it.

Leaving the hospital and being able to function in some way is really the most one can ask for the briefly hospitalized patient. And it is indeed a worthy objective. In such a case, the very best anyone can do is to arouse in the patient a curiosity about himself, which may lead to his seeking continued help. Any patient who is hospitalized for depression requires such continued treatment.

If, however, the patient can recognize the depression as a serious impediment to his development and sense of well-being, and wants to do something about it, you can proceed with the second move and ask the patient what he can do in this regard. It is in this setting that the trainee can make the many suggestions he is fond of making. And let me quickly add that it is necessary, in some cases, for them to be made.

However, the manner in which he makes the suggestions will determine whether or not his patient will be able to use them constructively.

Questions

When discharge is imminent and the patient starts to speak of getting a job, the therapist need not suggest, "You'd better go out Monday and find one." The urge to be direct and forceful is quite strong, for the hospitalized patient is so resigned that the young, eager therapist often feels that only a bulldozer will move the patient. That may be so, but there are many ways to bulldoze, if that is your bent.

To place a suggestion in the form of a question is not so very difficult. Some workers complain that there is no difference between making a suggestion as a declarative sentence or as a question. I disagree for two reasons. "Go find a job Monday" leaves the patient little option. If he says yes, he may feel he's made a commitment he cannot fulfill. If he says no, he feels guilty, and more of a schlumff than before. "Are you going to find a job on Monday?" leaves him with a greater option. If his answer is no, the door is not closed, and one can explore the advantages as well as the disadvantages of the *no* postion. If his answer is yes, a similar exploration may take place.

I want to emphasize that an explanation of the advantages of a *no* position does not infer that the *no* position is being condoned. The therapist is accepting what was just stated. He is only exploring, because he does not really know if the patient can do it. If the latter cannot, and failure is imminent, there would be no point in forcing the issue.

The second reason is that the patient is often unaware of the so-called leading question. While you may respect your patient's intelligence greatly, you need to know that the psychiatric patient's ability to discern seemingly obvious approaches is often severely blunted by his general alienation. If this is so, then the therapist may take advantage of the simple procedure (using question form) in order to help the patient feel he is arriving at the idea himself. Quite often, such patients will say, much later on, "I remember that you never told me what to do." It is good that the patient has this feeling, for he may thus develop a sense of autonomy which he could not otherwise.

I want to pause a moment here to state that this technique cannot be used exclusively. I am not indicating that the patient is asked what he wants in every situation. The hospital staff usually tells the patient what he is going to eat, where he is going to sleep, when he will be getting up and going to activities, etc. Even here there may be small choices, but if the patient were in the position to make all these decisions himself, he might not be in the hospital at all. Such questioning, like any other technique, must be appropriate to the particular situation and is by no means indicated in every instance.

A hallucinating patient, who was being discharged, was contemplating getting himself a car. It was felt that the patient was in no condition to drive. Yet one could hardly stop him. The patient had a driver's license, and the money to purchase a car.

The therapist felt he should say outright, "I feel I must advise you that in your condition you should not be driving at all." He thought it over and asked, "Do you think you should be driving in your condition?" The patient replied, "Why shouldn't I?" the doctor then asked, "What will you do if one of your visions appears while you are driving?" There was a pause, and then the patient smiled and answered, "I guess that wouldn't be such a good spot to be in."

If the patient had not responded in this manner, the therapist knew that he was prepared to state unequivocally that the patient should not drive. Furthermore, he was prepared to inform the family of this and, if necessary, the Motor Vehicle Bureau. Subsequent events proved this course unnecessary.

Indirect Questions

Where the patient cannot enter into a discussion about his intentions concerning his own pathology, the indirect questioning approach may be used. "Beatrice, what do you think Jane (who is also depressed) thinks about her condition?" In this once-removed position, it is often likely that Beatrice will tell you what she thinks of her own condition. As she describes what she thinks is Jane's position, Beatrice may be making connections, conscious or unconscious, which may have value for her. A whole line of questioning in this manner may be followed; "What do you think Jane ought to do—about getting an apartment? . . . . returning to her family? . . . . seeking treatment?", etc.

I am not going to include here anything about techniques designed to help the patient discover the roots and motivating force of his depression. But I am not suggesting that the first-year trainee should not use such techniques. Something of this will be discussed later on.

The procedures which have been described here are only a few of the many possibilities; they are never mutually exclusive. Now one is used, now another, depending upon its relevance. A collection of techniques may be regarded, in concrete terms, as the many spindles on a loom for a rug. They are all there and available, and each is introduced into the pattern when the time is right. The therapist is the person who knows best (but sometimes not so well) why he uses one or another at a particular time. This is why treatment of each patient is unique. No one pattern of approach is ever exactly like another. Planning, training, experience are all elements of the work, but none of them replaces the potential for originality which the psychotherapist and his patient share.

CHAPTER VI
A View of Self-Hatred

Self-Regard

Illness is a complex entity consisting of symptoms and defenses, levels of anxiety and depression, malfunctioning of interpersonal relationships, history of intrapsychic and intrafamilial conflicts. Running through it all is the quality of regard the patient has for himself, which in every case is poor indeed. A bland understatement, to be sure, but one which will be expounded upon.

If, therefore, I were forced to state the single area in which the patient most needs help, I would unhesitatingly say that it would be his regard for himself, above all else. Can we not say that as the patient's view of his level of adequacy or competency—in a word, his sense of self-worth—changes for the better, his symptomatology, defenses, and poor relationships would undergo change also?

The varying components of illness are dealt with exhaustively only to lead the way ultimately to feelings of greater self-worth. For example, a discussion of the symptom of agoraphobia has no significance in and of itself, except to point out that the patient must feel so weak, insubstantial and inconsequential, and therefore dependent, that he cannot trust himself to be out in the open where a potentially threatening world might decimate him.

As he grows in feelings of substantiality, he feels less dependent, therefore less threatened, and therefore more able to move about. Essentially, his new sense of self-worth offers him a wider choice—to be out and open to possibility, as well as to remain in and closed off to everything but his own survival, as he views it.

"Loving"

Development of a kind regard for oneself, then, is a goal of all psychotherapeutic endeavors, whatever the theoretical approach, technique employed, personality of therapist or patient, depth of illness, earlier experiences with therapy, or previous history. While it may be that a change for the better in a patient's index of self-esteem will not necessarily rid him of his defenses, symptoms, and destructive forms of behavior, it is nevertheless critical to all successful therapy, for it will at least help him to feel more comfortable with himself, even though those around him may not.

The part you have in achieving this goal goes beyond "loving" the patient and empathizing with him. Occasionally, it can be noted that the therapist "loves" his patient inversely as he loves himself. I stress the *occasionally*. This phenomenon, when it does occur, derives from the therapist's need for experiencing some form of genuine (in his opinion) affection. He does not concern himself with the transiency of such a relationship or even its untenable and inappropriate characteristics.

Where the above obtains, it must be emphasized that it is an extreme. No reference is being made to the warm, affectionate regard many psychotherapists have for their patients, and which is reciprocated, if erratically, by many of the latter. One can assess the non-neurotic character of this relationship by observing the therapist's ability to "take" his patient or to "leave" him, depending upon the exigencies of their relationship. Whenever the patient can experience a positive regard, he feels "good." Feeling good affords him a momentary release from feeling "bad," which is the way the patient usually feels about himself.

To digress for a moment, there is the tale of an analytic

patient who repeatedly complained that his analyst was not helping him and that he had spent a fortune over a period of five years. One day, the analyst asked him, "Why do you keep coming here if you are so dissatisfied?" The patient replied, "Because I like the way you smile at me when I come in."

Distortions

The patient manages to create one or more of several problems regarding the therapist's positive feeling toward him: (1) failure to recognize it, (2) inability to believe it, (3) elaboration of false meanings, and (4) inability to maintain the experience. In the first instance, the patient has had limited experience with true caring feelings, and he may not know that people, other than family members, can have such feelings toward each other. If he has experienced them in the past, his present pathology may not permit him to accept them at face value and so he remains ignorant of them.

Even if the patient recognizes your concern and care as such, he often tends to doubt that there is any sincerity or consistency behind these feelings and can only believe that it is "just part of the job." If he does accept them as genuine, he may go to another extreme. In his fantasies, he may embellish them with extraordinary false meanings. When he finds his false beliefs to be unfounded, he invalidates the entire relationship, leaving himself with the belief that the other's concern was only a sham.

Such an experience tends to reinforce his disbelief in the possible existence of any good feelings directed toward him. Because no one could, therapeutically, meet the exorbitant demands of his patient, the latter must reach this point of disbelief sooner or later. While the patient will seem to listen to reason, there is little the therapist can do under these circumstances except weather the storm and persist in his efforts.

Insight

Patients may have, upon occasion, a therapeutic experience in terms of insight; however, there is usually little or no carry-over. Whatever understanding he seems to have is most often limited to the moment of its occurrence. While you may never forget a significant insight on the part of a patient, the latter's depth of involvement as well as memory are not to be relied upon. This is not because of capriciousness or lack of ability to understand. It is because the patient is so burdened by anxiety and his need to maintain his defenses against it that he is much too distracted for the occasional blinding flash of insight to be more than just that—a flash. But this flash often blinds the therapist to the fact that his patient is not going to make rapid strides forward now that he has had such a profound insight!

Virus of Self-Hatred

Each of the four reactions to positive feelings has to do with the initial premise—the poor regard the patient has for himself. His disbelief in anyone's ability to have a kind regard for him is completely realistic if one starts from *his* premise. It is almost impossible for the inexperienced worker to appreciate the extensiveness of the patient's degree of self-hatred. This feeling pervades so many areas of his life, in such manifold ways so particular to him, that seldom indeed can he resort to one of his *islands of health* to support himself and mitigate his sense of hopelessness.

A small incident illustrates how even the nonpatient is inflicted with the "virus" of self-hatred. One evening, a famous composer and pianist had just played his last selection in a concert. The audience burst into applause. Coming off stage, he was congratulated by those in the wings. He spat out in German, "I played like a pig!"

It is unlikely that this great composer and virtuoso played like a pig at any time in his career—that is, your pig or mine.

But it is clear from the statement that anything less than the ultimate peak of performance, in his own particular terms, was a disaster for him.

Everybody knows intellectually, even the immortals of music, that not every performance can be *the* greatest. Yet it is the fear of that possibility that causes so many of the finest performers to drive themselves relentlessly and to make no allowances for anything less than perfection.

But how does one guarantee that one's performance will live up to expectations? There is no way. Therefore, the performer's efforts lead to his driving himself mercilessly, often subjugating all other areas of his living, all other relationships to this end. Excellence on the platform is the only meaningful experience for him. All else is ashes, and the great artist with such a drive is left alone with his art and his self-inflicted torment, relieved only transiently by his moments of glory.

Inner Dictates

For him, then, there is no *range* of possibilities. He can accept only one outcome. All other outcomes, fully acceptable in our terms, are remanded to the extreme of unacceptability and even hatefulness. This performer cannot say—I played superbly, or very well, or quite well, or not as well. He is caught between two extremes. His performance is either great or it is pig-like. Since the latter is unacceptable, he is left with no alternative but to be great each time he steps onto a platform. He has his orders from within. There is only one way to perform: "BE GREAT!" If he fails to be "GREAT!" one aspect of his inner self acts the raging, frustrated dictator who permits no deviation. He has only the one chance. He is rotten, deplorable, despicable if he falls short. Only unqualified excellence will restore him to the graces of his inner dictates, which remain ever relentless.

Some patients see a parent in the role of dictator;

however, by the time they come to the psychotherapist's attention, they have incorporated this view within themselves, and it has become part of them. Such an occurrence explains two things: (1) why patients have the same problems whether their families do or do not pressure them, and (2) why the therapist's feeling that responsibility rests entirely with parents does not help the patient very much.

Unless the latter can share responsibility in early adulthood for the elaboration and maintenance of his inner dictates, he can never deal with them, nor diminish their impact. He can only cry that mother or father made him this way (which may very well be true) for the rest of his life.

Please note, incidentally, that little can be done to wean the hospitalized patient away from such a view. There is just not enough time in most cases. All one can hope to accomplish is to relieve the pressure by accepting his "blaming" the parents. One need not accept explicitly—only tacitly, by not opposing the patient when he is able to bring his wrath down upon his parents. Explicit agreement from the therapist often must be paid for too dearly later on. Each therapist must know that this is a measure to be used gingerly, and only if it serves a calculated purpose.

Patient Standards

Between the artist and his critic there is usually a reasonable degree of concurrence. Excellence is excellence for both, more or less. In most instances, however, there are significant differences in the nature of the standards which a performer posits and those that the patient sets for himself. The patient's standards are usually uniquely his own, derived from a complex of interpersonal and intrapsychic experiences.

As with the performer, the principal feature of the patient's standards is the way he is led to hate himself when he falls short. But often the latter is immediately protected from the ravages of this self-hatred, as well as against the real or imagined threats of an external condemnation, for he is insistently prodded away from the position of his despised image. "Look, you despicable fool," he hears within himself, "look to your standards! You can do better than that!"

In this way, a spurious hope springs eternal. He will not only leave the "lower depths" but attempt to fly to the very heights established by each set of standards. When a pinnacle is attempted unsuccessfully, he is back to his "salt mines," from whence he soon begins to think he can once more zing his way to the pinnacle. Back and forth the process goes, keeping the patient in a hotbed of rapidly alternating heights and depressions. This is only one reason why the patient may find the quiet, often uneventful, therapeutic hour such a respite. On the other hand, for the person who would die of boredom in an anxiety- and conflict-free existence, this hotbed serves as a lifesaving vehicle. Something for everyone!

Conflict

To restate it, the patient's standards serve as defenses against his inestimable sense of worthlessness, even while driving him there. His involvement in this conflict does not resolve it. His standards are like so many tall, paper posts, surrounding him in irregular, concentric circles as far as the eye can see. He has one for every possible encounter with his world. He can never reach a top, because when he starts to climb one, it crumbles beneath him and he quickly scrambles to an adjoining one.

The process is endless, for he does not realize that he could knock them all over with his fist and have no further need to strive to mount them only to have them fold under his weight. He is so caught up in his compulsive need to rise "to the top" that he cannot appreciate the utter absurdity of his position; but he does experience the fruitless struggle, the wallowing in the depths of self-reproach, the shame and hopeless despair of not getting away from those depths.

The patient describes that state as "feeling like a worm under a rotting piece of wood." He cannot stop the activity, because he believes that it defends him against settling for a worm-like state. Because a worm-state is so unbearable to him, he must continue his eternal scrambling, knowing in his heart that it cannot work, yet unable to stop. A pretty hell indeed!

Strengths

In frenzied activity toward his spurious standards the patient encounters, scattered among his paper posts, some small mounds of substance which he has, willy-nilly, erected during his lifetime. These mounds of substance represent any true effort the patient has ever made, any true satisfaction he has ever achieved, any moment of joy, pleasure, or affection he has experienced—anything which once contributed to a brief sense of well-being.

Because those mounds may not be conspicuous or imposing, the patient overlooks them, forgets them, feels they are in the past, insignificant and not capable of assisting him in his climb to the top. They are, however, his strengths, his unrecognized reality. Reference to them will help him get out of the depths. Because the patient can neither recognize nor consider them, the therapist must keep a sharp watch for them, and help the patient to bring them into awareness when he learns of them.

These are the strengths which can give the patient a sense of self-worth and must come from within his own being. The therapist cannot manufacture these strengths. He can only help to place them within the reach of the patient, officiate at the union of patient and knowledge, and in this way lessen an alienation between the patient and his inner striving and unexplored potential.

For the hospitalized patient, a sense of externally derived

worth is usually necessary, as is any indicated medication in a medical case. But after the medication has had its desired effect, it is the inner resources of each patient that will insure his continued survival. The cardiac patient, who depends upon continuous medication for survival, can never go it alone, and is dependent upon his physician all of his life.

Similarly, the psychiatric patient who can never develop any measure of self-worth and autonomy is dependent upon someone for the rest of his life. While the cardiac remains irrevocably dependent, the psychiatric patient's state of dependency may range from extreme dependence, to dependence with occasional flashes of independence, to varying degrees of independence. His position on this continuum is determined by his inherent strengths, his incentive for change, and the effectiveness of therapy. Even schizophrenia, a chronic condition, has remissions as well as exacerbations; a five percent improvement here may mean the difference between lifelong, recurrent hospitalization and a life free of future hospitalizations.

"Superiority Complex"

Another view of the patient's rapidly oscillating "backs and forths" is observed as a seeming "superiority complex." If one hates oneself for one's inadequacies, how can one ever feel superior? This can be understood best in terms of the patient's self-imposed demands. While he may hate himself for not achieving perfection according to his standards, at the same time he maintains the prerogative of believing that the standards are the best there are. While he is "a stupid pig" in his view, at the same time he is patting himself on the back for having such superior standards. He comes to believe that many other people are "idiots" because they seem to be satisfied with little in order to experience a sense of well-being.

This seeming sense of superiority can be further understood when one recognizes that to regard oneself with contempt and hatred is so insufferable that the patient must resort to some ideal view of himself in his imagination to take him from the position of self-hating. With effort, this can be accomplished, so that the patient can endure himself at all. Life itself is not compatible with a completely unremitting, unrelieved sense of self-depreciation and worthlessness.

If the patient believes that he is nothing and can do nothing (always according to his standards), his fantasies come to the rescue. He must believe them, precisely because they have no grounding in fact. The weaker he feels, the greater effort he must make to have you and himself believe in his fantasy. He must continuously hide from himself the depth of his sense of nothingness. Awareness of this is what makes him severely depressed, suicidal, and often results in hospitalization.

Case Illustration

An extreme case of this very point is the following illustration. After a lifetime of psychiatric illness, a thirty-year-old, single, paranoid, schizophrenic patient was readmitted to the hospital because of a fixed delusion that a young woman in his office was in love with him but was too timid to tell him so. He was therefore determined to win her and had terrified her with his attentions.

That he had a good intelligence was unmistakable; yet he tested in the low normal range. He was tall, well-built, and could have been considered attractive, had he not been plump, or had such a guarded look about him, or such a bizarre way of speaking and behaving. If one listed this man's assets, one would find many—intelligence, youth, potential attractiveness, sensitivity, vitality, physical strength, stamina, industry, persistency, employability, optimism. His liabilities have already been mentioned.

When the patient was six years old, an "eminent

psychiatrist" had told his parents that the only meaningful recommendation he could make would be to have them send the child to live with a family with a different style from theirs, and far from the city in which they lived. Furthermore, he was willing to find such a family, who, in his opinion, would provide the warmth and kind, consistent concern that this child had never experienced in a family ridden with daily, hysterical outbursts, paranoid relationships, and common violence threatening to life and limb. The parents were insulted and took the boy home to complete the job. It was not their intention to do so, but they could do nothing else. Poor as it was, this was their best.

Because of a lifetime of failure in all relationships, including school and work experiences (he could not remain in school or keep jobs, even though he could always get one), this intelligent young man could not but sense, on some level of his being, how very limited he was and how empty his life.

Choices

What does such a person do when he begins to view his utter impoverishment? Most of the choices are not great. He can shoot himself. He can knuckle under and resign himself to a life of unrelenting mediocrity and deadness as long as he can make a living (this is where many people dwell). He can feel terribly abused and put upon, and project his difficulties on to the outside world (the extreme of this view is the murderer). He can withdraw and do his "own thing" proficiently, but without the joy of satisfying relationships. He can become the super-pleaser or martyr and feel alive only in the shadow of someone regarded as strong and decisive. He can become grandiose and invest himself with imagined abilities and a unique specialness. He can go into long-term treatment, with the hope that he can grow to accept his limitations, reduce the alienation between himself and his assets, and achieve some small measure of well-being. Patients usually reflect some combination of these possibilities. Whichever are to predominate depend principally upon the character structure of early significant figures.

Glorified View

This young man viewed himself as a composer-pianist, having written a musical play which he pounded out incessantly on the ward piano. It was delightful to witness his enjoyment of his rather poor playing. But it was saddening to know that he expected great things of his work in a public sense.

Writing was also a pleasure for him, and he had deluged his love with poetry. But his work didn't merit the public acclaim which he insisted upon. He filled page after page with bizarre drawings which were scoffed at by the other patients. He interpreted their indifference to his "genius" as ignorance, and the lack of appreciation of his resourcefulness as envy.

Everyone else in the world was unaware. Only *he* knew. With the help of his family he had developed a remarkable and persistent grandiosity. This was his defense for survival. For him, the only alternative to his imagined greatness was a most abject and insupportable view of an incompetent, inadequate, miserable failure who did not feel that one single thing about himself was in the slightest way worthwhile.

This was one way his intelligence and sensitivity had served him—to occasionally touch his impoverished position in the world. But, as mentioned earlier, he kept this view from consciousness by the constant elaborations of an acceptable (for him) image. Nothing less than the extreme of genius could atone for the other hatred extreme. Even though neither one had any real existence, he had made one his only reality. That being the case, his stance of grandiosity is understandable. This process is similar in any neurotic person, only the extremes are not as distant from each other.

The Promise

If the patient is lost in his attempt to make something substantial of a paper world, how can he ever be helped? What will he have to cling to? What will support him? What will nourish him so that he can survive his lunatic endeavors?

The first-year trainee often believes that he is the patient's support, and that if he allows the patient to cling to him, the latter will be strengthened. This is a difficult fiction to dispel, and I suppose it does not really matter, for two reasons.

Firstly, the inexperienced therapist will not disbelieve it in any case, primarily because it has elements of truth in it. *Elements.* Secondly, the patient does not cling so much to the person of the therapist as such, or to his kindness, or his patience. He clings to what is implicitly promised, and that is a belief in the strength of the patient. To the extent that the therapist holds out this promise, he will seem indispensable to his patient, who cannot himself hold the belief. The latter borrows his therapist's to support and to heal himself.

That is one of the reasons why patients who seem to be so dependent upon "my therapist" often make an astonishingly rapid shift to another "my therapist" when the first is transferred off the floor. The wrench is sometimes greater to the therapist, in whom a measure of health permits the establishment of a connection that has elements of genuine caring, affection, and concern. He feels the loss more deeply, because he has indeed lost something unique, irreplaceable, and rewarding, to whatever extent he felt that he was being of service.

The patient, on the other hand, often assumes that any therapist holds such a belief in his strength, and he can, therefore, accept the services of any qualified person. This is what he needs to think to allay his anxiety; one person is as good as another for this purpose. Few briefly hospitalized patients can respond to one therapist with any constancy.

Even when they can, it is no loss for them when a therapist's tour of duty has to terminate the relationship. The generation of even a slight positive feeling has already enhanced the patient in some small measure. This is the patient who will find you years later when he runs into difficulty again.

Separation

Another few words need to be said about the *myth of the indispensability* of the therapist. A difficult period for all occurs when vacation time comes around. The trainee who believes in the myth begins to become anxious about his departure weeks before the event. He feels that he must get the patient "ready," not realizing (1) that the patient's self-hatred leads him to believe that the therapist does not "like." him, and this will obtain regardless of any possible readiness, (2) that the patient can rarely ever get ready for something he does not like (nor can many people), and (3) that he is dealing primarily with his own apprehension concerning his absence and is, in fact, trying to ready himself.

I cannot go into the complexities of the trainee's own conflicts and anxieties about leaving the institution to which he has become attached and upon which he is dependent. But, whatever the genesis of his feeling, some of its elements are transmitted to the patient. Added to his feeling about himself, the therapist also conveys to the patient his doubts and fears about the latter's ability to stand up without "my therapist."

Brevity

The preparation of the patient is best handled by an attempt to arouse the least anxiety. Four points might be kept in mind regarding such an attempt. (1) In seeing others taking vacations, leaving the service, or terminating their terms of service, the patient is fully aware of the impermanency of the therapist-patient alliance. He chooses not to think about it perhaps, but he is well aware of it. (2) Some time before the departure, the trainee can mention (in context) and casually (if possible) that, in November, he will be going off the service and that such and such plans have been made for the continuing therapy of the patient.

Brief but forthright answers (including "I don't know") to any of the patient's questions can be given at that time, but no lengthy, anxiety-provoking discussion needs to be held. (3) Nothing need be said until several days before his leaving, except to answer questions as they arise. The therapist does not deliberately avoid talking about his leaving, but he avoids bringing up the subject himself and indulging in fruitless discussion. Beginning a session with, "Well, how do you feel about my leaving?" is practically like saying to the patient, "You should really have some profound feelings, probably negative and anxiety-provoking, about my leaving, and I'm sorry that I have to go, but if we wallow in your supposed anxiety a little while now, maybe you'll feel better later after I'm gone." (4) It takes perhaps five to fifteen minutes to explain plans to the patient about his temporary or permanent transfer to someone else. Should the patient bring up the separation over and over, the same responses can be repeated over and over, but *briefly* and with the attitude that it is already finished business. The patient will undoubtedly take the hint if it is given. It is not a kindness to keep the patient dangling with a subtle, implicit promise that perhaps the therapist can continue to see him even though the schedule calls for other plans.

Dispensable

Quite possibly the procedure outlined above may also be of use in the case of the long-term hospitalized patient, for here the therapist may feel even more strongly that he is abandoning his patient. In addition to the suggested procedure, however, the therapist is urged to consult his own feelings in this matter and to discuss with his supervisor what he would like to do. Sometimes, one's own unadulterated inclinations are the best guide for dealing with the psychiatric patient. Such a possibility can be tested only through one's own experience.

The problem of separation is handled easily when the therapist actually believes that he is not the only one on the staff who can treat the patient. Learning this early in one's career spares one a good deal of apprehension later on when it is necessary to refer a full practice to some colleague in order to take a jaunt over the bounding main. Upon discharge, a patient who had been in treatment for several years said, "*I* don't feel I can make it. But if *you* think I can, I suppose I can." And she did. The promise had been kept.

CHAPTER VII

Hostility Toward the Family

Hostility as Cure

One often reads or hears that the patient is "cured" when he can express his hostility openly. Because of that, the student inclines toward the belief that this is an essential goal of all psychotherapeutic intervention, including treatment for the hospitalized patient.

I would suggest that the student retain some doubt with respect to this matter, especially concerning the hospitalized patient. There are several reasons to warrant that attitude: (1) it may take a very long time for the patient to begin to get to the point of expressing hostility, if indeed he can ever get there; (2) there is no unanimity among therapists of different "schools" that this is an appropriate end point; (3) it may boomerang unexpectedly. (The expression of hostility, *per se*, is not the issue at all. An unskilled therapist may succeed in eliciting a great deal of rage from his patient; however, he is often not in a secure enough position to cope with it after it has surfaced.); (4) the goal of expressing hostility is often confused with the goal of being open and honest in expression (it is *not* the same thing); and (5) the goal of expressing the way one feels, reacts, etc. is the direction in which psychotherapists try to move, but such expressions need not necessarily be in hostile terms, either toward the therapist or toward any significant person in the patient's life. A goal, then, is not an expression of hostility but of trust leading to honesty and frankness. How close a beginning trainee can get to realizing this goal is not a matter for speculation here.

The goals of treatment for the hospitalized patient, especially for the patient who remains in the hospital for only a few weeks, are necessarily different from those for the patient to whom psychoanalytic techniques apply. Recognizing limitations of short-term hospitalization, should the trainee then deliberately attempt to acquaint the patient with the full impact of hostile feelings toward family and encourage him to spew forth that hostility?

This has been common practice among some beginners. They are generally delighted when the patient comes in and reports, "Did I let them have it when they came to visit!" Even when the therapist decides he should not be explicit about his glee, there is hardly any hiding it; and the two have a little mutual congratulatory session. That is not an outstanding accomplishment, however, and I daresay that a large percentage of psychotherapists have had this experience in their first year of training.

Hostility as Feeling

On the positive side, there is something to be said for an expression of hostility against the family—when a patient comes to this point himself, without the therapist's prodding. It is a new and nonthreatening atmosphere in the therapeutic relationship which permits the patient a little easier access to his inner thoughts.

An anxious, depressed, self-effacing patient was very dependent upon his domineering schizophrenic wife. She wanted a divorce and he believed that he loved her deeply. Seeking information, and without innuendos, the therapist asked him what he liked about her. The patient was at a loss to answer the question and finally revealed that he did not know. Initially, he seemed slightly amused, but later had a difficult time with this revelation. In therapeutic sessions, the patient became furious with his wife as he recalled the signs of disinterest and neglect and the innumerable episodes of ridicule and humiliation he had suffered at her hands. He could not resolve the dilemma of supposedly loving her and yet have these new feelings. Fortunately, however, the wife insisted upon her freedom and the story had a happy ending.

Often, the patient who comes upon a new set of feelings, so blatantly in contradiction with another set, is thrown into irresolvable conflict because he is not strong enough to take the necessary measures to dissolve the partnership. This patient was eventually able to relinquish his wife, thereby experiencing a tremendous relief. His depression diminished, he returned to work, and finally entered into a marriage with another woman who seemed not to have the extent of pathology that his first wife had.

Even though it may be short-lived, a sense of relief is a welcome respite from anxiety and depression. That is especially so for the person who has been terrified of the impact of his own hostility. Knowledge that an expression of hostility does not rend himself of his family may leave him with a sense of confidence or, at least, a moment of euphoria, which may be the only bright spot in an otherwise grim existence. Experiences of this nature may clarify aspects of relationship to the family. It may even serve as the beginning of a search for the truth of his predicament. Certainly, such an outcome is all to the good.

Who Can Stand It?

Can expression of hostility toward *anyone*, in or out of the hospital setting, excluding family, accomplish the same end? Is it mandatory that members of the immediate family bear the brunt of a patient's struggle to free himself? Is it possible that encouragement of such expression may ultimately result in pressures with which the patient is in no position to cope? Should a psychotherapist consider his course judiciously before deciding to afford his patient relief at the expense of the family? Can someone else with whom the patient is less emotionally involved serve the purpose? I want to repeat that it is not expression of hostility per se that is at issue here, but overt expression of hostility specifically toward family.

On the positive side, there is also the possibility of the patient's experiencing a brief sense of power. This could occur if he succeeds, momentarily, in dumbfounding his family and seizes, in a flash, the significance of their incompetent expressions, before the full impact of the outrage hits them. Even a moment of vindictive triumph can serve as a significant release for the depths of despair in which so many patients dwell. However salutary temporary release may be for the patient, it has to be recognized for what it is. When the patient has this experience, and shares his triumph with his therapist, he often gets to feel that the latter is really plugging for him and is on his side, as opposed to the family's. I would like to insert here the following question: *Could it not be regarded as more therapeutic if the patient felt his therapist and he were aligned FOR rather than against something?*

Definitions

Hostility and anger are often confused. A brief excursion into the meaning of hostility and its relationship to anger may, therefore, be pertinent here. According to the dictionary, hostile feelings encompass ill will, malevolence, a desire to thwart and injure, enmity, unfriendliness and animosity. Synonyms include hatred, rancor, vindictiveness. Anger is usually regarded as a strong passion or emotion of displeasure, and as antagonism, excited by some sense of injury or insult. Both anger and hostility may be expressed or unexpressed. They may be conscious or unconscious. Hostility contains, also, a large component of fear, which may or may not accompany anger.

Persistent fear is never, in my opinion, absent in the hostile person, and, in fact, serves to distinguish the hostile person from the merely angry one. The hostile person often looks frightened. The angry person, who is also fearful, usually looks more angry than fearful. Depending upon the character structure of the hostile individual and/or the circumstances at a particular time, either the anger or the fear will be more in evidence at any given moment.

While anger and fear may be uncomplicated and transient responses to a simple or uncomplicated provocation, there is nothing simple about a hostile state. Finally, the hostile person may be said to be a permanently angry and fearful individual who has stored away the fears, hurts, insults, resentments, and angers of a lifetime and clutches them to his breast as an essential, protective, life-maintaining shield. There is such strong, even violent feeling invested in hostility, that one often feels compelled to inhibit its expression at all costs.

Overt Hostility

When there is enough pent-up anger and fear present to cause a patient to feel hostile toward family, certain questions may be raised. Would it be destructive to be the agent who releases the stops which control the pouring out of such feelings? Can young workers take this responsibility upon themselves? Are they in a position to safeguard both patient and family from uncontrollable mutual vituperations? Should the release of basic anger be at all encouraged in the short-term, hospitalized patient? Are there other ways of relieving the patient without the family being blasted by a newly "freed" patient?

An expression of overt hostility toward family, especially parents, can have extremely untoward outcomes.

Regardless of the family's attempts to understand, be patient, and cooperate, it must be recognized that it probably has a low threshold for tolerating further evidences of the patient's pathology, family therapy notwithstanding. At the risk of sounding contradictory however, some families do have remarkable tolerance for old, familiar patterns of pathology and resign themselves to it. Such a family, however, is in no position to tolerate new forms of behavior which could be hurtful and frightening to them.

New expressions of hostility on the patient's part would be classified by the family under new forms of pathology rather than new evidences of strength. It would have no ready-made defenses for them. While the family might be taken aback temporarily, and give the impression of accepting the new-found courage of the patient, it often comes back, after getting a so-called second wind, and is furious with the patient for taking advantage of a seeming patience and forbearance.

In private therapy, it is at such times that parents snatch their offspring out of treatment, and husbands refuse to pay for their spouses' continued visits to the therapist. While the latter may be congratulating himself for having helped the patient speak up to his family, he may at the same time be losing the patient, or, in the case of the hospitalized patient, he may have alienated the family even further from its weakest and neediest member.

Dependence

The dilemma inherent in this position is that the patient is really very dependent upon the family. To do anything which enrages and discourages family members further, and which gives them additional reason to reject the patient once again, is not serving the patient's needs. Unless the therapist can bring about a permanent separation between the patient and a destructive family, which is neither likely nor realistic, he does well to maintain the good offices of the family in as many respects as possible.

In most instances, the short-term psychiatric patient returns to live in the family home. He has little choice if he is not strong enough to "be on his own." This being on one's own is fraught with obvious pitfalls. Even if the patient has the strength to find work himself and a place to stay, he may feel too isolated and depressed to remain alone. It can be surmised that such a patient gains more than room and board by remaining with his family. While there might be mutually destructive relationships in the home, there is at least the opportunity for some interaction which, in some cases, is better than no interaction at all. In some ways, human beings require relatedness as much as they require food. It would be folly to work to separate patient from family, unless a more desirable alternative could be found; even a quasi-facsimile for living is preferable to a lonely, if peaceful, emptiness. Incentives for constructive efforts would be at a minimum, or nonexistent, in the latter, while they might be more pressing in the former.

Alternatives

Since the trainee is in no position to take the patient into his home and provide for him in every way (despite some fantasies to the contrary!), and since he would do well to limit stringently his expectation of the family's tolerance to "go along with" the results of his earnest therapeutic endeavors on behalf of the patient, and since there may be no other alternative, he must tread cautiously when working to effect separations from family, for he may be unwittingly leading the patient into a path of isolation, self-neglect, depression, and suicide. This does not mean that a given patient would not be better off away from his family. He may very well be, but the circumstances must be calculated to be supportive.

There are many such circumstances with which the therapist can familiarize himself. There may be relatives willing to put up with the patient. The expression "put up with" is used advisedly because it would be uncommon for a psychiatric patient not to be a difficult person with whom to live. There may be a group of patients, discharged at approximately the same time, who might live in the same apartment house or nearby, so that some interaction could be maintained. Several patients might be able to room together and share expenses and company. This sounds almost idyllic, but each is usually so demanding and difficult that these partnerships seldom survive. (Junie Moons are the exception.) There are residence buildings specifically for single persons, who can have privacy or company, whichever they desire. The problem here is that patients too often tend to remain in their own rooms, and become withdrawn anyway. Halfway houses and community centers are fine, but only if utilized by the patient.

In view of the difficulty of finding a suitable place for the patient to live, alternatives have to be considered. If the patient's hostility toward his family has been made manifest to them, there is always the possibility that higher levels of hostility and tension will exist in the home. Again, I repeat, that doesn't have to happen if family members can be helped to understand what is going on, are constantly supportive and supported, and have the patience and fortitude to withstand pressures. However, such families are the exception, and planning for this outcome will not make it so. Even under ideal circumstances, where the family's intentions are the best, they cannot be expected to understand the patient's needs which make such urgent demands upon them. Furthermore, even when the family seems accepting, there is always the possibility that they may be unconsciously undermining and vindictive. That risk alone militates against a tactic leading to the expression of overt hostility.

Besides having to deal with the shortcomings of his family, the overtly hostile patient has now to deal with his own self-rejection and growing guilt for (1) recognizing such hostility in himself toward the family, (2) making the family feel more angry and distressed, (3) hating them even more for making him feel guilty, (4) hating himself more for hating them, and round and round it goes in a vicious cycle.

The hospitalized patient cannot tolerate added pressures, even though a sense of pressure is nothing new to him. Anxiety levels tend to rise, and because they become so intolerable, depression often sets in, for the depressed state is more tolerable than an increase in anxiety. If the patient tends to be on the manic side, he may become more so. In other words, there may be an exacerbation of any symptom which serves to bind the anxiety.

Limitations

One can be of greater service to his patient if, while sympathizing with him, he can help him to appreciate his family's limitations. With *selected* patients, questions like "Do you feel that your family deliberately tries to make it hard for you?" may be useful. While such a question may elicit a reaction of greater guilt (remember the patient is already guilt-ridden), it may also have a salutary effect in bringing to the patient's attention the fact that perhaps his family is not out to get him. Regardless of some families' propensity toward schizophrenogenesis, one would be hard put to say that any one pair of parents sets out consciously to induce schizophrenia in their child. Nor, indeed, could any spouse be so accused, unless he had some morbid desire to wish his partner out of the way.

While it may not be salient, many psychiatric patients often have a minor component of paranoia in their thinking. Because of it, they may regard, without good cause, friends and family as out to do them in. The question above helps selected patients to reorient themselves to another possibility. The consideration of another view of his family might help the patient to *accept* (not like) a family he hates, yet upon whom he is totally dependent. A secondary gain is that, in even a slight acceptance of the limitations of an admittedly impossible family, the patient may inadvertently develop a minuscule acceptance of his own limitations. Even a small change here certainly constitutes a considerable gain.

Realistic Goals

The deliberate eliciting of explosive expressions of hostility is best reserved for the times that the therapist is continuously available to the patient. At such times, the homeostasis of all relationships is threatened, even that of the nursing staff and other patients. They become agitated when someone becomes acutely anxious or when he becomes overtly hostile. While even violent hostility cannot always be avoided, I am addressing myself only to that behavior which results from the efforts of a zealous therapist, with every good intention of helping his patient to become autonomous. A worthy objective to be sure, yet one has to decide whether or not such a goal is a realistic one for the short-term, hospitalized patient being treated by the inexperienced, transient trainee.

CHAPTER VIII

Islands of Health

Alienation

I have repeatedly indicated that it is helpful if the psychotherapist can guide the patient to discover his own strengths. These have been referred to earlier as the patient's *islands of health*. Their discovery, on the patient's part, leads to a diminishing of the patient's condition of alienation.

That truth can be ascertained. If the patient has a strength (island of health) to which discovery he must be led, then he has obviously not been aware of it—a clear sign of alienation. If it can be discovered at all, then it is there and does exist. If it exists and the patient is not aware of its existence, especially if his being aware of it could help him in his growth, then obviously he is disconnected, or separated, or alienated, from one of his resources. One can assume then that an extensive pathologic structure must lie between the individual and his resources and potential.

Regardless of intensity of pathology, and seeming absence of any resources (health), the novice can make an assumption that buried in the morass of illness there are some islands of health, however small and tenuous. The only generalization to be made regarding that particular point holds true for most patients—that there are, in all probability, some of these islands. What they are, how they can be recognized, and how the patient can be guided toward them is in the nature of the therapist's work. Whether or not they are aware of it, whatever their therapeutic stance or jargon, all psychotherapists must attempt the discovery of these islands, or their service to the patient is of limited value.

What Is an Island?

What are these islands of health? Frequently stumbled upon unexpectedly, they constitute a body of surprises to both therapist and patient. Occurring throughout the patient's lifetime, they may be encountered at any point therein, but are most frequently found in early life. They may be a distant, faded memory of a once briefly known person, a photograph, a trip, a special occasion, a pet, a friend, a poem, a song, a moment of triumph, merriment, beauty, repose, or grief. They inhabit any place, person, or thing toward which the patient has had the slightest positive authentic feeling.

The positive feeling may not be detected initially because of depression and a sense of despair. The patient does not shout to us, "Now listen carefully, because here is something that I have at least a modicum of good feeling about." Whatever it is, it can only emerge as the patient is encouraged to talk, to tell us about himself in all respects, about all phases of his life, not just about his illness and its history, with its various embellishments and ramifications.

If a man has been a stitcher of furs, it may seem to the un-initiated that there is little here that is related to his pathology or that can aid in his recovery from an acute illness. Yet, if he has that skill, you must recognize that he is certainly an experienced workman. If you come from a background which could not possibly help you understand, then one would hope that you could become sufficiently curious to explore new data. Your curiosity informs you that you know nothing about "fur-stitchers." If you give the patient a chance, you will soon know a good deal about that craft.

Intriguing the Patient

The trainee's position is an enviable one. For here you are—young, eager, intelligent, curious, and nonknowledge-able. What a jolly combination! There is little you could not learn if you seize the moment of learning. Awareness of your ignorance, plus curiosity, leads you to ask, "What does a fur-stitcher do?" The patient may regard such a question with contempt: "Imagine anyone not knowing what a fur-stitcher does." Or, he may further deprecate himself: "Of course, why should anyone know what a fur-stitcher does? Who is a fur-stitcher anyway? A nobody." Nevertheless, he might take the bait. Perhaps he cannot resist it. How often does a tired, discouraged, depressed old fur-stitcher have the opportunity to tell an eager, intelligent, curious young therapist all about fur-stitching? Never! This is the first time it has ever happened. It may never happen again. This does not mean, however, that the patient will launch into an exposition of his craft simply because you asked a question. But don't forget that he has that bait rolling around in his mouth. Neither of you may know it. But it's there. He may not believe that you want to know about his work, but you have given him a start, helped make an opening for him merely by asking.

Curiosity

This is a critical moment. If you are truly curious, you will have little difficulty in conveying your interest. If you are not curious and are just going through the motions, the patient may or may not respond. I cannot say how successful your attempt would then be; something would be lacking. There is always the possibility that your interest might be aroused if he kept on talking, for here is something you had never heard of and might listen to with some interest, because it is so very new in your experience. Fine! It does not matter how you arrive at an attitude of genuine curiosity or interest or openness, as long as it is achieved. Sooner or later, most patients respond to the therapist's interest, whatever its form.

Your initial response, whatever the piece of data, is a vehicle by means of which the patient feels a degree of acceptance. It's a kind of "love me, love my dog" phenomenon. The patient who listens to you profess an interest or concern, but who feels that you are not interested or have no curiosity about his means of livelihood, has reason to wonder about the quality of your care. The therapist who feels he must attend only to the element of illness in his patient had best pause and question the value of this approach.

Referring to his curiosity, the novice may say, "Well, I don't really care about the old fellow's fur-stitching, (quarrying, farming, fishing, accounting, whatever) and I'd feel like a phoney if I pretended to be interested." Interest and curiosity are not the same thing; but it might be said that interest is a sustained curiosity about something. One need not feel he has to go all out in being curious about something. We can be transiently curious about the most dull or trivial of happenings. This curiosity will enable the therapist momentarily to focus with such intensity and direction that the patient may seize the moment and respond with some measure of aliveness. Thus, relying solely upon an ability o expose his own curiosity, the inexperienced therapist can have a healing effect upon the patient.

Nourishing the Patient

It cannot be emphasized sufficiently how hungry the patient is for this kind of human response. Up to the point of his experience with you, other people (friends, family, etc.) have tried to tolerate your patient. They have had difficulty accepting him because his illness is frequently too much for them. This is understandable, for psychiatric illnesses lay a heavy burden on family and friends, regardless of their efforts and good intentions. The message many patients receive from those closest to them is one of rejection   and good riddance. The patient has probably not had the experience of being listened to wholeheartedly, without impatience, for some time. Such attention is the basic nourishment of existence and, as such, a major ingredient of therapy. This is why therapy starts the moment the first-year trainee sits down with his first patient and asks, "Will you tell me what brought you here today?" He may be quite anxious when he asks this question, but he wants very much to know, if for no other reason than that he has to tell his supervisor something. Whatever your motivation, the patient grasps the urgency of the need. This is a fresh, welcome breeze for him and he is often willing to be taken along with it.

As you exploit your own desire to learn, your curiosity, your wish to help by exposing yourself to the patient, he is held intrigued by it all, even though he may have strong doubts about its being of any value to him. The patient does not know it, but the moment he is intrigued, he is being helped, regardless of the extent of illness or the therapist's competence. Most patients will not be intrigued by the disinterested, noncurious, covertly rejecting   therapist. Fortunately, the presence of such personalities in psychotherapy is uncommon.

Clues

The point has been belabored, but only to underscore the fact that a particular piece of data is not the important factor. I could not possibly list even a fraction of the most common islands of health in most patients. What is important is the belief that they do exist, in all patients, and in a multiplicity of variations.

How, then, does one recognize any of these variations when they arise during an interview? There are little clues which the patient is always dropping. "I used to go roller-skating years ago." The expression "used to" is the clue here. It may very well be that the island of health revealed here relates to this patient's ability to roller-skate. We aren't certain yet, but it's worth a little detour. "Oh, you roller-skate?" "Not anymore." Silence.

The patient may continue with his roller-skating if the therapist does not say anything, because silence leaves an opening. If the last thing he said concerns the skating, it is unlikely that he will talk about icebergs in the next sentence. Although it is probable that he will continue with skating, it might even be, "No, not since I broke my leg in the early 60's." Don't be discouraged. "Had you done much skating before that?" or, "Where did you do your skating?" etc., etc. Of course, all this may not work. What you are hoping for is an entry into one of these past memories where you and your patient may stroll leisurely, letting him lead the way, while you point out the direction. If he will not move into the opening you have occasioned, another opportunity may present itself at another time.

Appraisal of Intellect

The patient's intelligence may be regarded as an island of health, if it has brought him some success. A quick appraisal can be made without waiting for tests or extensive interviewing, by asking the patient two or three simple questions. "How far did you go in school?" The answer to this question should be evaluated on the basis of the socioeconomic background of the patient. The middle-class patient who has completed the 11th grade may be in a different category from some foreign-born patients who completed the same grade. To the latter, it may have represented quite a significant accomplishment, in view of economic and cultural pressures upon him to leave school as soon as he was old enough to find work. This question in itself, however, gives limited information.

The next question is somewhat loaded and requires most careful observation to interpret the answer. "How did you like school?'' The answer must be carefully evaluated in the complete context in which it is given, including the tone of voice and facial expression. When people like something, they often smile. While the patient's pathology may not permit him to smile, you may have to search for clues of feeling in what the patient says.

The next question is even more loaded: ''How did you do in school?'' No one likes to say, ''I was a miserable student and couldn't seem to learn anything.'' But you still want to know if this is so. On the other hand, self-effacing patients may not be able to say, ''I did extremely well.'' After waiting a reasonable time (and some patients cannot answer this question at all intelligibly), you can add, ''Did you usually pass?'' There are three fairly standard replies to this question. The good student says quickly, ''Oh yes, I always passed.'' The average student says, ''Yes, I passed,'' but without the same alacrity. The poor student says, hesitatingly, ''Most of the time,'' which might be untrue, because he may have failed most of the time. But it is not critical; you have already gleaned important information.

If you have decided that your patient was a fair or good student, you can readily ask, ''What was your average?'' Feeling that your questioning his academic achievement is no threat, for you asked only if he passed, he will tell you that he had a C+ or D average. If he did better, he will be quick to tell you, permitting you to make your evaluation. The poor student will be reluctant to give information and should not be pressed on this score. If the purpose of such questioning is only to make a quick estimate, then your purpose has been achieved. The patient's poor school performance can be investigated more fully subsequently, with a view to understanding the total personality.

This fairly accurate method of assessment can be accomplished in about two minutes. If there is a significant discrepancy between the information (i.e., poor academic history) and the therapist's personal assessment of the patient's intelligence (very high), then this is important data and an additional indicator of pathology.

Intelligence as an Island

For the patient who did well academically, a large area is now open for exploration. There will be many satisfying experiences that the patient can relate and inadvertently feel good about. However, you must take special care here to avoid two possibilities. The first is to become so encouraged with the patient's ability to function intellectually that the latter feels he is being pushed to achieve. If he could really function, he probably would not be your patient. He can easily feel coerced by your enthusiasm. A sense of coercion makes him so resistant that even if he should attempt to function academically, his resistance might very well insure his failure.

All the information the patient imparts must be listened to as impartially (but attentively) as one listens to information that the patient's grandmother made apple pie with nutmeg instead of cinnamon—surely nothing to celebrate, to encourage, or discourage. It does not mean that the therapist is unresponsive! I am only trying to indicate how you may inadvertently make your patient feel called upon "to perform" before he is ready to do so. Not only will his fear of failure make him more anxious, but he will unconsciously avoid relating such events to you because the outcome will be painful. Thus, a valuable opportunity will be lost. You will not then be able to draw upon the patient's constructive experiences as a delicate straw bridge leading across the abyss to health.

The other situation to be avoided is the possibility that listening to the patient recount his successful academic experiences might result in the patient's feeling worse about himself because he is not able to achieve similarly at the present time. This outcome would be more likely in the case of the patient who still has academic aspirations that he has not been able to realize. In that case, such an exploration should be avoided. It could be more safely used with the older patient whose school experiences are well behind him, or with the younger patient who is no longer involved in this kind of striving. The rule of thumb would be to watch the patient's reaction as he relates his story. If he seems fairly comfortable with the information he is relating, then the therapist can take the risk. If the patient seems to get excited or euphoric, it might be unwise to continue until this line of exploration could be discussed with a supervisor.

More Clues

The therapist who uses his eyes and ears to the utmost will not only hear the verbal clues but will also hear the implicit clues manifest in change of tone, pitch, and speed of delivery. He will note obvious changes in expression, and the less obvious vasomotor and respiratory changes. As the patient moves toward something about which he has felt "good" at one time in his life, there will be many subtle changes in his person. Changes can be observed, not for verbal noting, but for encouragement. As the therapist becomes convinced that he is pursuing something worthwhile, his patient catches the mood and is willing to pursue the subject further. Each one propels the other as they explore a little island together. The entire operation may take only a few minutes or the entire session. But a successful exploration has delineated for both yet another small island. It may never be referred to again by either, but it will continue, nevertheless, to nourish the patient as he continues his search for wholeness.

CHAPTER IX

The Doctor-Patient Alliance

This section was prepared especially for the physician-in-training as psychotherapist. There are certain features of his experience which have to be pointedly emphasized so that he will make full use of them. However, many of the points made here obviously apply to all beginning psychotherapists.

Definition

The *doctor-patient alliance* is a relationship established between the doctor and his patient, from their very first meeting, to initiate and to expedite a possible healing process. It is a useful and comfortable cooperative and aims to preclude the introduction of certain interferences to treatment. In medicine, the patient who will pull an IV infusion needle out of his arm has not entered into the alliance. In psychiatry also, the patient may not be willing to take his medication, or he may refuse to see his therapist or talk with him. Ideally, the doctor-patient alliance is a "two-way street," but the doctor can initiate his part in it with or without the patient's cooperation. With time, however, the persistent therapist can usually effect the necessary changes to ensure that it is the reciprocal alliance it is meant to be.

Therapist Limitations

The doctor-patient *relationship* has been described repeatedly in the literature. Reference is made to the doctor's warmth, acceptance, empathy, freedom from anxiety, and so forth. While the tyro therapist is not told explicitly that he should be wise, a tower of strength, and serve as the repository for the patient's devastating anxieties, fears, delusions, etc., he nevertheless often believes that he should possess these characteristics from the early days of his work. Intellectually, he knows that this is impossible. But that knowledge may be of small comfort, for his unconscious demands upon himself dictate that a therapist is a therapist and that there is no excuse for being less than an effective one. From such demands stem the psychiatric resident's feelings of incompetence and the belief that he cannot be of any "real" service to his patient.

Fortunately, these feelings are so often tenuous and quickly dissipated by the novice's tendency toward optimism and/or grandiosity, that he bounds easily over to the side of hope and faith. In this state of mind, he can be of greater assistance to his patient, because no patient profits from negative proclivities; he has enough of his own. Ironically, the very ignorance of the inexperienced therapist is a strong factor in the maintenance of optimism. Indeed, if he were to realize how little he could help his patient, he might become discouraged. In time, however, as he learns to appreciate his limitations, he realizes that the little he can do is often of great service in moving the patient toward discharge and toward some degree of autonomy in caring for himself.

As the therapist begins to recognize the gap between the existing situation and the ideal goals of a doctor-patient relationship, he may despair. Only if he is in good health can he learn to live with and accept (without malice toward self) a gap that is realistic and inevitable at this stage of his development. It would seem, then, that undue emphasis on the "good" doctor-patient relationship, early in training, may be self-defeating—for, as has been noted, the healthy young psychiatrist will develop a basic sense of confidence despite a recognition of his many shortcomings. Even if it is true that the doctor is not capable of developing a so-called good doctor-patient relationship, he can effect some kind of *alliance* from his first meeting with the patient.

Elements of the Alliance

Every therapist knows that some kind of workable rapport must be established as soon as possible because certain expectations must be fulfilled. The patient is suffering. He has come to the hospital to be relieved of his suffering. He expects to be relieved. His family expects it. Hospital personnel expect it. The physician expects to assist in this task. Usually, the patient is expected to help also.

The purpose of hospitalization is fairly clear to all concerned. That indicates to each member of this expectant group his assigned task. The psychiatrist-in-training must examine the patient physically, establish his mental and emotional status, take a history, make a diagnosis, and decide on an initial course of treatment. These are fairly routine procedures for which his prior training has prepared him and left him, hopefully, with some sense of competence. In the practice of familiar, routine procedures, the physician is least anxious. He knows his way with these.

Thus from the earliest contact with the patient, the doctor has entered into a *doctor-patient alliance*. One might say that it is predetermined by the routine quality of the necessary tasks performed under the aegis of treatment. There has been no need to concern himself with his sufficiency to enter into such an alliance. It is established, ipso facto, merely by his and the patient's being there together. The doctor-patient relationship, in a psychiatrically meaningful sense, is a much more intricate and delicate entity, and by its nature depends largely upon the background, experience, personality, sensitivity, motivation, and goals of both doctor and patient.

Essentially, the doctor-patient alliance requires that the doctor meet certain basic criteria in the care of his patient and that the patient be available to him. Anxiety and uncertainty are diminished as the doctor learns to appreciate the importance as well as the inevitability of this alliance—and more, that he is quite capable of commencing it immediately. No one asks that he be an effective psychotherapist; nor is he pressured to establish a so-called meaningful relationship. That is something which may evolve in time and with his further growth as psychotherapist.

Common Interests

Initially, therapist and patient have purposes and goals in common. Usually, the patient comes to the hospital and is admitted in order (1) to relieve distress, (2) to prevent self-destruction, (3) to effect removal from an intolerable milieu, (4) to relieve family tensions, (5) to prevent further disintegration, and (6) to receive treatment.

Patient and doctor may anticipate (1) preparation for discharge from the hospital with new, tolerable levels of anxiety, (2) maintenance with or without drugs and outpatient therapy, (3) some level of functioning and a return to a familiar milieu, (4) remaining out of the hospital, (5) more autonomous involvement in therapy, and (6) a growing sense of well-being. Such shared hopes and goals certainly make for a commonality of interest.

Doctor and Patient Resources

The patient contributes whatever personal assets he has to this cooperative work. He also brings his confusions and suffering, together with an inordinate resistance and a profound fear of change. What he really wants is to be "patched up," to feel well again. For the most part, he is not interested in a serious investigation of etiology or in gaining insight into his problems. Nevertheless, his need for relief makes him accessible to the ministrations of the doctor, and the latter utilizes this.

Besides a sincere wish to relieve the patient, the doctor brings much to the doctor-patient alliance. Among the personal assets are his training as a physician, his life experiences to date, his intellect, vitality, interests, enthusiasm, humor, curiosity, and a capacity for compassionate concern. Without this last, the psychiatrist may work effectively with his patients, but often a vague sense of dissatisfaction will surface. As one matures and develops that capacity, he frequently comes to feel that he is making a startling discovery in the realm of doctor-patient relationships. But finally, he recognizes the "discovery" as something that many of his colleagues may have been experiencing for years.

The Unavailable Patient

Sometimes the patient will not cooperate with the doctor and not appear for the psychotherapeutic session. It is the psychiatrist's obligation to find a way to persuade the patient to come or, failing that, to visit the patient. The doctor has the obligation to find out what has kept the patient from psychotherapy. Patients may fall into two general categories when they will not avail themselves of treatment. The first includes those who may find it impossible to do *anything* constructive on their own behalf. The etiology of this condition can be uncovered only by meticulously reviewing the personal and family history, where one will find an uncommon quality of vicious neglect in repeatedly undermining words, deeds, and attitudes on the parts of all significant family members.

The second category has to do with the patient who is "turned off" by the doctor. If the doctor wants to know about this possibility, he might go to the patient and say, in effect, "I've come to your room because I want to find out what has kept you from coming to my office." If the patient cannot respond to this, the doctor might continue: "Is it physically difficult to come?" "Is it frightening to come?" "Are you too angry (too sad, too disinterested, etc.) to come?" "Do you feel that it is no use—that I cannot help you?" "If so, then perhaps we can try to find out how I can."

This can be conveyed to the patient without a "true confession" that the doctor is inexperienced and that the patient has to help him in order to help himself. While this may be true, the patient is not particularly interested in all that. Very often, such frankness can result in arousing the patient's contempt for the doctor. The patient thinks that he is in the hospital because he is unable to care for himself, and now this "joker" is telling him that *he* doesn't know how to care for him either!

Perhaps this point is unclear, but there *is* a distinction between (1) conveying the fact that it is desirable for the patient to cooperate, if possible, in the process of therapy and that the therapist has his limitations, and (2) spelling out the idea that he (the therapist) is an inexperienced, incompetent person who hasn't the foggiest notion how to go about helping his patient feel better. More important, the last is not true. Visiting the patient to find out why he is not coming to treatment sessions is one way of helping the patient. Should one of the questions be pertinent, the patient may feel some small relief, believing that his doctor knows why he couldn't come, overlooking the fact that a question rather than a statement was posed. That the doctor did not know which question was applicable is something the therapist can keep to himself. There is no need to burden the patient with that truth, for while he can accept certain limitations in his therapist, he is usually made more anxious by the latter's admission of bewilderment, incompetence, confusion, and anxiety. Such revelations may be appreciated in an open encounter situation where everyone exposes the full extent of his "hang-ups" and inadequacies. But the hospitalized patient is not a good candidate for this form of treatment. Nor is the beginning therapist the one to conduct such therapy.

Therapist Arrogance

Patients are sensitive to many facets of the doctor's personality and feelings. Not fully aware of the doctor's shortcomings, they tend to be quite forbearing. However, they tend also to be exquisitely sensitive to qualities of impatience, contempt, and arrogance. The psychotherapist may regard such feelings as cardinal sins in himself or in anyone else; nevertheless, they may very well be present to some extent.

Of the three, arrogance is probably the most deadly. It is this quality which "turns off" the psychiatric patient most readily. The patient senses it; he fears it; he admires it; he cannot cope with it; he despises it; he has no use for it; he wants to be arrogant also. Obviously a conflicted response!

Arrogance has, through the ages, been equated with strength. Even today, some people still feel this way. In our culture, signs of real or imagined strength are greatly admired (e.g., the making of instant heroes out of certain types of lawbreakers). The patient is a child of his culture and often cannot help but feel the same. At the same time, a show of arrogance belittles him, derogates him, renders him weak—the loser. How, then, can he admire something which renders him impotent? He must despise it, fear it, hate it, rid himself of it, have contempt for it. But, if he does that, then he is dealing the death blow to the very quality that he wants for himself—one way to feel strong and in control. Even though those positions may be unconscious ones, a seductive quality to the latent possibility of the latter is irresistible, and he is torn between his admiration and his fear/hatred. And so the cycle of conflict is generated and maintained.

When a psychoanalyst arrives at a point of conflict in his analytic patient, it is grist for the mill. The first-year psychiatric resident, however, does well to remember that he is not a psychoanalyst, nor is his patient an analytic patient. While in all probability attempts will be made, such a conflict cannot be dealt with effectively. Direct approaches by an inexperienced person to a patient's conflict may throw that patient into greater conflict. Such an outcome is not desirable, for anxiety is increased and symptoms exacerbated. I repeat, unless one is prepared by training and design to deal with such explosive material, it is not wise to rush in.

But how can the inexperienced worker know whether or not he is arrogant and what the effect will be on the patient? A difficult question, because the psychiatrist with an arrogant component in his personality often has opposing components as well. The latter may blind him to his arrogance, for he may feel that he is always kind and accepting, especially with patients. While this may be true to a point, it does not exclude the other possibility. So where does the doctor stand whose arrogance is turning off the patient and who is completely unaware of it?

The supervisor might be able to help the doctor start to question which of his personality characteristics or feelings may be interfering with his alliance with the patient. This could prove difficult with the therapist who is not in treatment himself. But as long as the supervisor is not too ambitious, some small inroads might be made.

Other factors might help the therapist to deal with certain of his feelings toward the patient. For one thing, the truly curious therapist is so attentive to the whys and wherefores of his patient, that more negative characteristics are kept from intruding. Since arrogance and curiosity are certainly not mutually exclusive, one's intellectual curiosity may serve as the connecting link between a patient and a doctor who tends to be unconsciously arrogant. A feeling of arrogance between the therapist and patient is an alienating factor for both; curiosity is perhaps one of the best defenses against such alienation.

Doctor-Patient Relationship

When long-term treatment is possible, the therapist must go beyond the doctor-patient alliance. He must become involved in a relationship which encompasses more than the procedure already described. Central to effective psychotherapy is the necessity for alleviating the patient's intense self-hatred. The *doctor-patient relationship* is the principal instrument to accomplish that goal. In supervision, one of the difficulties of dealing with that relationship is that one can only talk *about* it. It is a discussion which is always second-hand, hearsay.

However such a discussion takes place, sensitivities are exposed. As this occurs, other facets of the doctor's being are touched as well. He begins to experience himself as a "warm body," in there with the patient and having mixed feelings and reactions. It is difficult to capture the essence of the exchanges which take place. To talk about feelings of warmth and concern almost divests them of these very qualities. How, then, does one teach or learn about a relationship which is crucial to a therapeutic outcome?

One may speak of openness. In order to achieve the goal of openness, one must set aside preconceptions which are obviously antithetical to openness. Such a setting aside permits the therapist to say, implicitly: *I accept you as you are, with all your defenses, with your limitations, gifts, resources, with your craziness, with your drive, energy, vitality, or whatever lack. Sometimes I am exasperated. Sometimes I like you. I do not like your psychosis, and I am sorry that you are troubled by it. But I accept it as one aspect of your being, for you are more than a mass of illness to me. The mere fact that you are human makes you a fantastically marvelous creature. There is no other being who can begin to compare with you in interest, versatility, complexity, and potential for continuous, constructive, or destructive development.*

I want to underscore that the first-year or even the third-year resident must be most tentative in verbalizing these thoughts to his patient, if indeed they are ever verbalized. Their impact is felt in much the same way that one conveys to a child that he is loved. When the feeling exists, the child knows it, and no explicit words of love need to be spoken. If one is genuinely concerned for the patient and wants to care for him to the best of one's ability, the patient will sense it. It is conveyed to him in dozens of ways—the way questions are asked, the words that are chosen, the tone of voice, the facial expression, etc. If the patient does not get the message, and it is there, it is only because he is too constricted and frightened to let himself have this form of nourishment. He is suspicious and guarded and cannot believe that something worthwhile is being offered him.

With regard to the doctor-patient alliance, however, the first-year resident usually fulfills its modest requirements. His curiosity leads him into the uncharted sea of the patient's pathology. The doctor's going through the initial steps of the alliance, together with his wanting to know, to find out, is therapeutic in a limited way for the patient. Remember, it is seldom that the latter is approached by someone who is not irritated, impatient, or filled with the self-hate of his own impotence.

Cornerstone of Respect

Finally, the success of the doctor-patient alliance rests on the cornerstone of respect for the patient's thoughts and feelings, his strengths and weaknesses, his fantasies and his realities. The psychiatric resident may feel comfortable with any patient if he remembers that in a morass of illness, there are many islands of health as points of reference. This latter thought brings to mind the story of the perplexed driver whose car had broken down in front of a psychiatric facility. Leaning out of a third-story window, a patient called down a workable solution. "Say," remarked the pleased motorist, "what are *you* doing in there?" "Well," replied the patient, "I may be crazy, but I'm not stupid!"

CHAPTER X

Notes on Suicide

Intention

Threat of suicide is one of the most distressing problems the psychotherapist has to face; and this obtains for both experienced workers as well as their junior colleagues. When a suicidal gesture or unsuccessful attempt has been made previously, the potential for suicide has been confirmed and makes further evaluation somewhat less soul-searching. But where history is lacking or is less than clear, one is strictly on one's own in making a decision about the possibility of suicide.

Sometimes an obscure *intention* of the patient must be uncovered in order to make the principal distinction between a suicidal *gesture* and a suicidal *attempt*. As the term is used here, intention refers to conscious factors. A bona fide attempt is *intended* to end one's life. While basic motivation may be complex, intention and the act are unequivocal; here, failure is accidental. Even when the move is seen as an impulsive act, intention at the moment of impulse is clear. Impulse attempts are often accomplished in the context of what is available at the time—pills or a window.

Planned attempts may involve high bridges, automobile "accidents," hangings, cooking-gas, carbon monoxide, and—the most common—barbiturates or other drugs. Any single one of these will suffice for the person bent on suicide. However, more than one means may be used, as in the case of a particularly enraged man who had lost his job, owed money, and had been cuckolded and deserted by his wife. He expressed deep self-hatred when he committed suicide by sealing off the kitchen, turning on the gas, stabbing and hanging himself.

A post-mortem determination of suicide is usually based upon the means employed, if there is no written statement. When the patient survives, he can be questioned about his intention. It is probably safe to assume that the more lethal the means, the more definite the intention to die. Once the decision to commit suicide is made, adequate means can always be found, for it is almost impossible to prevent the suicide of a determined person. Emphasis in therapy, therefore, must be focused on reducing the virulence of self-hatred, so that determination lessens.

Intention of the individual who makes a suicidal gesture is a many-faceted affair. In general, the intention is not to kill one's self, but only to have a brush with death, in order to arouse some new feeling within one's self or within another. Perhaps the most common intention is to utter a *cry for help*. Teenagers or young adults who believe that their parents are deaf to their pleas and blind to their distress, feel that only a dramatic move will bring them to attention. As is often the case following a suicidal gesture, parents are aroused to want to *do* something—to change the youngster's school, to move, to take him to the doctor, to a hospital, anywhere, with cries of "Why didn't you tell us!"

Orthodox parents, after exerting pressure on a nineteen-year-old son who wanted to break away from their orthodoxy, were terrified, perplexed, and furious with themselves when he swallowed a bottle of aspirin and was hospitalized as a psychiatric patient. Their remorse knew no bounds even as he admitted that he knew the aspirin would not kill him. "It was the only way I could think to get you off my back!"

It is likely that unconscious forces are responsible for the gesture which accidentally succeeds or the attempt which accidentally fails. An understanding of these forces is sometimes beyond the scope of the novice and can only be assumed by the experienced worker, always subject to confirmation by the patient.

Gestures

There is the patient who becomes intrigued with the notion of death, and wants to experiment peripherally with it. He takes several pills with the knowledge that someone will find him shortly, or that he might be in a coma for awhile, but will eventually awaken. The feeling of intrigue is central to his intention. It is a flirtation which gives him a sense of power (if only fleeting), of control, of a cynical but martyred abandonment. His perverse enjoyment in tantalizing himself is more desirable than a feeling of absolute nothingness.

A twenty-five-year-old woman was hospitalized because of "repeated suicide attempts." She was diagnosed as schizophrenic, and no examining physician could find any strong evidence of suicidal behavior. It was finally discovered that she had "slashed" her wrists upon several occasions. Detailed description of the slashing revealed superficial cutting of skin "on the back of my wrists, because feeling the warm blood flow down my hand made me feel alive. Otherwise I felt so dead. When I didn't have a razor, I'd use a comb. But that didn't work very well. All it did was scratch the skin." While there was evidence of these "cuts," no scars were ever noted. In her torment, the patient would often cry out that she wished she were dead, but would later admit that she had no intention of doing away with herself, and has not made any move to do so for many years.

Hysteric

The so-called hysterical personality frequently uses threats and gestures to control his environment, because he feels so helpless. He learns early that if such control is exercised, he feels more secure. Unfortunately, he "cries wolf" too often and control lapses. He then becomes unbearably frustrated and may go too far one day in an attempt to reestablish his position.

A fifty-five-year-old woman lived on the top floor of a tenement. When she felt that her family was not giving her enough "respect," she would announce dramatically that she was going to throw herself from the roof. She would then run to the door, fling it open, pause, and wait for the family to capitulate, which they did. One evening as she made the announcement, her husband raced to the door before her, threw it open and said, "Let me help you dear." She burst into tears and fled into her bedroom. Several days later she was found unconscious on the neighboring roof, some ten feet below the roof of her building. She revealed later that she had never really intended to kill herself, but, having been humiliated by her husband, she wanted to "show him" and "punish him" so that "he'd be sorry." Furthermore, if she had succeeded and died, "it would serve them right!" A woman of her age could have been killed or seriously injured in such a fall. Suicidal? Your move.

Revenge

Among lovers, passionate revenge accounts for many suicidal gestures, as well as attempts. It is surprising how many beautiful and talented, but morbidly dependent young women, having one lover after another (always the current one to be the "only one"), run the risk of suicide following the humiliation of rejection. At first, they insist that they really wanted to die, and one is hard put not to believe them. One can accept this, because the humiliation, the sudden loss of support, the isolation, loneliness, and subsequent anxiety are certainly intolerable.

Yet, a remembered fantasy before the act reveals an exquisite corpse lying in a flower-strewn casket, deeply mourned by a repentant lover. As his hot tears touch her face, her lids flutter open. His love has brought her back to life! He falls to his knees, vowing never to leave her again. She smiles gently. All is forgiven. Curtain.

The suicide gesture, as an act of vindictiveness, often succeeds because of poor planning. Distraction, caused by intense anger, may account for an accident. The victim forgets that his roommate had told him that he would not be there that night, and therefore would not interrupt his dying as had been expected. Or, he forgets that tomorrow is Saturday, and that no one will think to look for him until Monday, and so forth.

Loss of Control

Financially successful persons who conduct their lives with some order cannot tolerate a sense of loss of control. They tend to plan a suicide attempt fairly well and usually succeed. When they fail, it is often difficult to determine what the intention was; sometimes, after all the facts are gathered, one can deduce its nature.

Such a patient, feeling depressed for several weeks and complaining that he was being a burden to his family, entered a hospital. After a few days, he left the hospital with the intention of killing himself by throwing himself off a bridge. Unsteady, he couldn't make the leap, and fell from the railing onto the roadway. His absence at the hospital was noticed almost immediately, also a note stating where he could be found. Everyone was fully convinced that he had intended to kill himself. But somehow his method was ineffective. Even if he had managed to jump, it was a low bridge and he was a strong swimmer.

The family rallied round and he was treated "with kid gloves" for many weeks. Remaining in a petulant mood, he enjoyed all the attention. Eventually he returned to treatment and made a fair recovery. The attitudes of the family seem to have been altered permanently, for they had indeed been impressed by his move.

Punishment

Some patients are furious with their failures and want to punish themselves, but with reservations. Some patients want only to retreat—to get away from it all—but only temporarily. They may take just enough barbiturate to remain comatose for twenty-four or forty-eight hours. There are those who hate some aspect of themselves and wish to be rid only of that feature. Although it seems reasonable to them at the time, it is clearly evidence of delusional thinking. In a more rational moment, they admit that their intention was to rid themselves only of the hated part, and they see the absurdity of such a belief. Such patients may make the most bizarre suicidal moves, and may be suffering from a long-standing schizophrenia.

Suicide Following Depression

It is sometimes observed in the hospitalized, depressed patient that the depression suddenly lifts. Experienced clinicians know that such a dramatic change is suspect. Their experience has taught them that this phenomenon may occur when the potentially suicidal patient has finally resolved his dilemma. He has decided that because there is no hope (in his terms) for him, he will put an end to his misery. Relieved by having made a decision, he appears much improved physically and psychologically. He may also be enjoying a feeling of triumph; he holds a secret trump card. Only *he* knows that he is going to be rid of his suffering, and he relishes this knowledge. He has something that no one else has. He bides his time, waits for the propitious moment. Then, several days later, he is found dead, either in or out of the hospital. The uninitiated are left with a sense of shock and frustration—"But he seemed so much better!"

Hospitalization

It is not a simple matter to tell a family that a member of that family must be hospitalized, forcibly if necessary, in order to protect him from possible self-destruction. One has to consider the possible trauma to the suspected suicide patient who is willing to be treated as an ambulatory patient, but who might lose all hope for himself were he to find himself incarcerated in even the finest facility. Yet, one is called upon to make this decision frequently in the course of a career. That probably causes him most of his sleepless nights, not to mention the spoiled vacation time when he is worried about either having left a patient "on his own," or having, perhaps unnecessarily, hospitalized him. Nevertheless, when there is an uneasy doubt in the therapist's mind, it is probably best to err on the side of caution, unless he can be immediately available.

Guidelines

The novice therapist is but one member of a team whose members he can generally consult on the question of suicide. However, when he is alone in the emergency room on a weekend or in the middle of the night, the exigencies of the situation often demand an immediate decision. Panic may cause a lapse of judgment, and a decision may be based more upon fear of error than upon the circumstances dictated by the case. Basic procedures are lost sight of and, therefore, cannot be relied upon to help diminish anxiety.

The therapist is provided with a wealth of literature and outlines of procedure for the admission of patients; many guidelines are available to him. Much time, thought, and talent have gone into the preparation of teaching aids, and they can serve the uncertain beginner well, if he will but avail himself of them. In this context I am reminded of the cartons of you-put-it-together-yourself objects which have stamped in bold letters across the top: IF ALL ELSE FAILS, FOLLOW THE INSTRUCTIONS!

Mental Status

A carefully administered mental status examination is an important aid for the determination of a potentially suicidal

patient. The ability to use this procedure as a specific tool
helps to uncover certain invaluable facts about the patient's
illness and may serve to diminish the therapist's anxiety,
thus bringing to the fore his own good judgment. Novice
therapists are sometimes squeamish about asking a
seemingly well-compensated patient if he has ever thought
of killing himself. They are afraid of putting the idea into his
head, if it is not already there. They also feel that it is almost
a derogation of the integrity of the individual, and do not
wish to be responsible for causing him any further distress.

Sometimes, one "forgets" to make the inquiry when the
patient does not appear particularly distraught. It is a disservice to the patient not to do so. It is possible, however, to
employ language that will preclude further trauma, to
gradually lead up to and elicit the information being sought.
Of course, it is essential to remember to ask in the first
place.

Most therapists have little difficulty asking about
frightening thoughts or dreams. That question may
immediately elicit the information one is seeking. When
time is limited, questions about dreams might be excluded,
for it can take one on a long detour, after which the novice is
in no better position to evaluate suicidal potential. Even a
terrifying nightmare with violence and/or dismembered
parts would be difficult for him to interpret.

After having determined mood, affect, etc., a dialogue
might proceed somewhat in the following manner.

"Have you ever had any strange thoughts?"

"Oh, no, doctor. I'm always so busy, I have no time for
anything like that."

"Like what?"

"Well, strange thoughts."

"What kind of strange thoughts?"

"No, I never had any strange thoughts."

"Have you ever had any frightening thoughts?"

"Oh yes, when I was a child. I was afraid of the dark.

After I saw scary movies, I would look under my bed, and I didn't want to go to sleep.''

"Did you have frightening (or bad) thoughts when you were older?"

The adolescent or young adult group, among whom the suicide potential is quite high, is often likely to have thoughts about suicide in connection with possible school failure or when alone on some weekend, their classmates having left the campus or being involved in some kind of fun. The depressed college student reaches his low on a weekend, especially when no one else is about and he feels his isolation most keenly. Such a patient may very well admit to thoughts of suicide in response to the question of frightening thoughts. The doctor may interrupt lengthy responses at any time if they do not seem relevant to the task at hand, especially when there is a pressure of time.

If all this reveals no evidence of suicide ideation, one can press further. "Have you ever hurt yourself in any way?" "How do you mean, doctor?" Pause. The patient may continue despite his question. "Have you ever hurt yourself when you might have avoided it, or have you ever *thought* of hurting yourself?" Some rather bizarre forms of behavior are often uncovered as a result of this question. Patients may reveal a history of lesser forms of self-destructiveness: a clawing at their legs, burning of legs and thighs with cigarettes, scratching or cutting of wrists with bobby pins or pieces of cut glass, generalized scratching resulting in weeping eczema requiring hospitalization, and so forth. If such information surfaces, it is not difficult to ask "Have you ever hurt yourself or thought of hurting yourself in a more serious way?"

Much might be revealed at this time—a thought, gesture, or attempt—unless the patient is deliberately trying to conceal such evidence from the examiner. The critical question to be asked at this point is, "Have you ever thought of doing away with yourself?" A surprised response to this is often revelatory. "How do you mean, doctor?" "Did you ever do anything to seriously threaten your life?" (One need never use the words "kill" or "suicide" if one has an aversion to them.) The chances are pretty good that if the patient ever took an overdose, or jumped out a window, he will remember it now, even if he has forgotten it up to this point. The middle-aged patient might be asked if he ever threatened his life as a youngster.

But why all the shilly-shallying to avoid the direct question, "Did you ever think of or try to kill yourself?" (Thinking of killing one's self is more common than one likes to think—always remember that there is a tremendous gap between the thought and the deed.) If the patient has, he will probably say so. However, if he has not considered suicide seriously, such a question could be dwelled upon by the suggestible person with possible infelicitous results. One has to be in a position to provide the necessary protection in case such a patient decides that perhaps it's a good idea to commit suicide. Should the patient ask, in an alarmed way, "Why do you ask me that question? Do you think I'm so crazy that I would kill myself?", the response can be a simple, "It's just a routine question every patient being admitted is asked," which is absolutely true! After all, who knows what thoughts lurk in the mind of the borderline suicidal patient when he is under stress? Promoting the idea of suicide when the patient never had such a conscious thought, may prove a hazard for the beginner.

Questions relevant to suicide can be asked and answered in approximately five minutes and *should be asked of all hospital admissions, and of most persons coming to an emergency room.* Such persons have usually reached their anxiety tolerance level; otherwise, they might not be there at all. Excluded here is that group of patients who come regularly to the emergency room as they might to a therapist for a little reassurance or medication. These patients are usually recognized by the permanent staff, who can quickly assess their status and offer suggestions regarding management.

Precipitating Factors

When one has determined that suicide ideation is present, one must ascertain, if possible, what the precipitating factors are. If such ideation or some attempt occurred in the past, one needs to find out what led to it at that particular time and then decide if present factors parallel those of the past. In other words, the doctor can use past history effectively to judge a current situation, keeping in mind all the other data he has obtained. Patients with a hysterical personality sometimes make a suicide gesture following the termination of a love relationship. If such a history is elicited regarding a previous termination, the risk is high that another such gesture may be made. It is crucial to remember that a percentage of gestures succeed accidentally. One cannot be casual therefore, in assuming that such a person would not *really* try to kill himself.

The *sine qua non* for a positive decision regarding suicide probably depends upon past attempts. Whatever the patient's degree of integration, such information should be carefully assessed in light of the age of the patient, relationships, time of occurrence, related circumstances, content of the ideation, time between thought and deed, method of attempt, etc. Even though you may feel it is uncomfortable for the patient to go over such a history, most patients find that talking to an interested person about even painful memories is not overly distressing.

Where the threat of suicide is a new one (crisis), and other factors have been taken into consideration, the quality of current relationships is an important factor. If there are dependable friends or family members who are tolerant of the patient's distress, who are not too anxiety-ridden themselves, who can be comforting and reassuring, who are willing to assume responsibility for the patient's welfare, and who are not floored when told that the patient is probably suicidal, it may not be necessary to hospitalize the patient, but rather to treat him on an ambulatory basis until the crisis subsides. *It is only fair to add, however, that such friends or family members are few and far between.*

A detailed history (if time permits) that reveals a background of healthy experiences and relationships and the experiencing of joys and satisfactions is a strong factor against possible suicide, even in the severely depressed adult. The implication here is that the history of some suicidal patients is marked by a paucity of constructive experiences. Yet, on the sudden demise of a seemingly healthy person, one frequently hears, "I would never have expected *him* to take his life!"

Examples of the latter have occurred among people who experience sudden, serious financial reverses or a humiliating diminution of personal prestige. A dramatic illustration appears in Allen Drury's novel, *Advise and Consent*. Senator Anderson, a successful, much admired, handsome young man, in a highly respected position, shocks the reader by placing a revolver in his mouth and killing himself. This can best be understood in terms of a precipitous fall from a position of power in which much pride had been invested. The Senator believes that his unblemished reputation is going to be besmirched by a political adversary's discovery of an unacceptable episode in his past life. That kind of person cannot afford any imbalance. The slightest push will shake his pedestal, and he will come crashing down to the bald fact of his fallibility. One who has created a myth of infallibility for himself finds this knowledge insupportable, and must go on to feel worthy only of extermination.

Price for Success

In such a case of sudden, successful suicide, the history of the present illness is the most revelatory. Unfortunately however, it is mostly hearsay. The attempt usually occurs only a short time after the real or imagined fall from grace. The past history of such a person may include many successes in school, work, and play. But investigation often reveals a success achieved at the cost of much tension, anxiety, and betrayal of self, especially in the case of public figures. The right series of moves have been made in an unbroken *chain* of events, each one carefully calculated to bring him closer to whatever goal he has set for himself. So much energy, talent, time, and attention have been given to the "project" that little is left for nourishing an inner sense of well-being and the need for closeness with others.

The individual in this position loses everything if he loses anything. For him, there is only one position to attain and maintain. There are no approximations. It is all or nothing. This is his principal defense. When something happens to diminish that position to any extent, the fall is inevitable and complete. The defense is shattered. To swoop from utter success (for in his mind this has been achieved) to utter failure (there can be no middle ground) is so overwhelming that psychic integration is shattered. "If I am not equal to God, way up there, then I am nothing anywhere else. I cannot tolerate this humiliation. I do not deserve to live." The decision is irrevocable. Bang! And the deed is done. These are the jumpers, the fatal drivers, the shooters. These are the perfectionists who believe in their perfection. They can rarely be stopped because they attempt and accomplish this last act with the same planning and perseverance that they have approached everything else; success is thus assured, and there is little time between the actual falling off and the act. No one suspects. There is no apparent deprecation, no decompensation or deterioration. Just the flash of knowledge that they are imperfect, and that perfection, in fact, never existed, cannot exist, and is forever beyond their grasp. Hence the hopelessness mentioned earlier. They can go from the pinnacle of success to self-destruction in a matter of hours or days. There is no dilly-dallying, no clues are given, no search for sympathy, no call for help.

One will have little experience with this group of suicide victims, because they rarely appear in the emergency room of the general hospital. Their decision is irreversible, and even the final act is doomed to succeed. They know that to fail would be too bitter a pill just then.

Depression and Suicide

In many cases, severe depression may precede the act of suicide. The quality of such a preexisting depression must be delineated. Questions leading to information about the nature of the depression must be asked—when, how long, how often, in relationship to what and whom, etc. One must try to elicit the cardinal symptoms of depression, among which are a sense of anger, guilt, loss, helplessness, and, finally, hopelessness. The suicidal person is ready to do away with himself because he has lost all hope of ever achieving the status he sees as his only salvation, his *raison d'être*. His disdain and self-contempt for having failed is towering and relentless.

If such an attitude cannot be mitigated quickly, then hospitalization is required to protect life and to gain time. Time is needed to help the patient restore a sense of pride in himself. This is often referred to as improving his self-esteem. But it is well to understand that true esteem cannot be developed during a limited hospital stay. In truth, a successful hospital stay serves to restore some measure of pride, concomitant with diminished self-hatred; the patient "feels better." A "patch job" to be sure, but it is all one can do under the circumstances. A more helpful service is provided by making the patient aware of the need for an investigation of his values and life style. This investigation is the focal point from which he will, hopefully, evolve new ways to fulfill his unique humanness, rather than a spurious facsimile of godliness.

Finally, it is my opinion that with very few exceptions (one exception would be the case of a prolonged, painful illness with a hopeless prognosis) suicide is a final act of culmination of intense, pervasive, excoriating self-hatred. So persistent a belief in one's unworthiness might be regarded as evidence of delusional thinking. For it seems that such a fixed, false belief in one's lack of potential for growth can be regarded only as a thought disorder, especially in the light of the extraordinary resources every human being—body, intellect, and senses intact—has available.

CHAPTER XI

History Taking as Therapeusis

Begin at the Beginning

Some years ago, I heard that young trainees at a medical clinic had to spend an entire year learning how to take a careful history. Impressed by this, I began to notice the general quality of psychiatric history taking. The range was a wide one. More conscientious workers took long, detailed histories, which included material gleaned from three to six interviews. Some completed their entire history taking in one interview and only added to their knowledge of the patient's history as information was presented during the course of the therapy. Few appreciated the wealth inherent in the accumulated data, or the opportunity it presented the patient to know, to touch himself in ways that he had not explored for some time. Nor did the therapist think of history taking as an initial phase of therapy.

Therapists and supervisors were aware that history taking (1) gave the inexperienced worker an opportunity to begin to establish rapport with the patient, and (2) contributed to the making of an accurate diagnosis. However, it was not regarded as a primary therapeutic tool. I believe that it can be used as such.

Alienation

There are certain features common to most psychiatric patients. It is well for the beginner to familiarize himself with them as soon as possible. One of these is often referred

113

to as *alienation*, an extreme of which is the phenomenon of depersonalization. Patients will refer to feelings of depersonalization (the therapist's term) as a sense of separation from self, from body, from mind: "I don't feel I have a core"; "I don't know who I am"; "I sometimes don't think that anyone can see me"; "My head seems to be floating above my body. They are not connected"; "I feel all the parts of my body are disconnected."

Lesser forms of alienation are evident in such remarks as: "I can't remember blocks of time in my past"; "I don't remember my father before the age of seven"; "Things that I remember seem to have happened to somebody else"; "While I learn things and get good grades, I don't think I know anything or that I deserve the recognition I receive"; "I can block anything unpleasant out of my mind"; "I don't ever feel enthusiastic or excited about anything." You are, of course, aware that the latter remarks may be heard from anyone, and not only from a psychiatric patient.

I shall not attempt to define alienation in a comprehensive way. Reams have been written about it. But I will say that it is a process having to do with the quality of one's relatedness to himself and to others. The alienated person may feel at a distance from any or all of his present and/or past experiences, including those related to childhood, adolescence, education, training, associations, memories, achievements, and so forth. Some of these areas are completely blocked out from awareness. Some are merely vague, some incredible. The term "unreal" is often used to describe quality of involvement. Absent is a firm sense of belonging, of ownership, of autonomy, of authenticity.

Alienation is an unconscious process; but some persons actually feel a lack of substance in their relatedness, a disconnectedness in areas of their living. Those most aware of that probably suffer more than those who have no sense of loss, no sense of peripheral living. Both groups may seek solace in some relieving compulsiveness (i.e., overwork, overplay, alcohol, drugs, sex, etc.)—or they may seek treatment. Those who do the latter are already on the road to whatever recovery they will eventually achieve. Their suffering provides them with incentives to seek help, and to make the necessary efforts to effectuate change.

Those who seek treatment, however, are usually not equipped to do anything that will influence a change in degree of alienation. Knowing what the problem is does not solve it. But the therapist can help with this by finding out the areas in which his patient is most alienated. He also needs to know that alienation can be reduced. It is his obligation to learn which first steps may serve to accomplish that purpose.

History Taking

Approaches must be explored; these should be compatible with the beginner's knowledge at an early stage of development. Sophisticated techniques are neither applicable nor effective when used by tyro therapists. History taking is something that can be taught in an orderly fashion; anyone should be able to learn how to do it. There is a graphic quality wherein the procedures facilitate learning. The history can start at birth, or prior to birth, and proceed year by year. Students can be provided with specific questions and procedures which can then be employed with the patient. Thus, a detailed autobiography may be elicited from the patient in response to the therapist's organized questioning. I am not describing an only way or a best way, but just one possible procedure.

A beginning worker may be instructed by his supervisor in the use of history taking as therapeusis under various circumstances. An anxious and/or inexperienced therapist is often at a loss for *content* in the session. He does not know the questions to ask, which comments to pursue, what points to emphasize: in general, what information is to be elicited. He does not know how to fill his time with the patient.

At times, the therapist seems at no loss for words. Yet, he finds that sessions follow a stereotyped pattern, with both patient and therapist repeating the same formulae, hoping for some felicitous outcome despite the repetition. Such an outcome is possible. However, it would not be the product of repetition, but rather the therapist's obvious concern for his patient.

The behavior of severely obsessional persons serves as an illustration for an extreme form of such repetitiousness. These patients have no control over their compulsions, which have evolved to free them from anxiety, but which invariably fail to fulfill that purpose. The obsessional patient then expects to be reassured by you and, thereby, relieved of intolerable anxiety. This, too, fails, for after you have given him the same answer to the same question for the umpteenth time, he is immediately pursuing the same round of questions. You are eventually rendered so distracted, feeling such impotence, that you devise ways to avoid your patient, shorten his sessions, and, finally, attempt to medicate or transfer this patient who cannot be helped by your best efforts.

Often, a patient is unproductive. He will answer any question briefly and simply wait for the next one, taking neither interest nor responsibility in a process that requires mutual cooperation. Therapists find themselves talking a great deal with such patients. The patient then becomes even more quiet and more disinterested. The therapist may then become angry, accusing the patient of resistance.

Severely depressed patients are most trying, for a relentless pessimism pervades their every act. They may be talkative or quiet, but their hopelessness is implacable. It seems that nothing you do or say will make the slightest impression. These patients are also difficult for experienced workers to treat. But the novice is often overcome by the patient's hopelessness and pessimism, and may come to believe with the patient that indeed there is no possibility for even limited recovery. In this state, you are not of much service to your patient. This does not mean that you abandon him. It means that you do whatever is necessary to restore your belief in the basic constructiveness and latent potential of human beings, even the most severely ill.

Interest Begets Interest

Although you may not have been reduced to incompetence by any one of the above conditions or others not discussed, you may decide to use the method of history taking as therapeusis. As your patient responds to your questions, and as you become more interested in those responses, his interest may also develop. He may find that his memory improves as he goes along. He becomes more detailed, more spontaneous. He may go off into other reminiscences which you could not possibly have discussed, having no inkling of their existence. His associations have taken him to a realm beyond the scope of your list of questions.

You are now practicing psychotherapy; your stimulus has enabled the patient to proceed under his own power. When he slows down and stops, you can help him again in the same way. Let him give you every nitty-gritty detail—of the first time at the circus, of a dog bite at age five, of the garden his father planted, of a neighbor who moved away. Let him talk and talk. He will get to enjoying listening to himself after a while. And you listen and listen.

Your patient is sending out a steady stream of tiny, very fine, invisible links between the self he presents to you now, and the experiences of his past life. Momentarily, feelings of separateness will necessarily diminish in intensity. You will hear, over and over: "I haven't thought of that in twenty years";"I had completely forgotten that happened to me"; "I never knew I felt this way about that," and so on and on. You are helping him to reconnect with himself, however the place or time is articulated. A form of reconstruction is taking place. Again and again, in miniscule steps, you are providing him with a vital experience. Reconnect—reconnect—reconnect. Much of a life that had been lost to your patient is slowly and painstakingly being dragged out of dark recesses and out into the light of an unencumbered present. Now he can inspect, consider, and savor it in his thoughts.

Everything Counts

Some therapists query only in areas of pathology. While such information may be useful, overemphasis here may be antitherapeutic. The patient must be led to make contact with other aspects of his history. Who, if not you, is to ask him about the rest of his life, about his successes, his satisfactions, his triumphs, his sweet memories? These will serve as the knots of a long, slippery rope in the process of health restoration. He will use these knots to lift himself out of the morass of his illness.

Your patient must be asked about everyting—good or bad. Do you remember your first day in the first grade? Do you remember your teacher's name? What did she look like? Did you like her? What kind of person was she? What did she like to do most in the classroom? What was her favorite story? What was yours? Your favorite song, game, activity? Did you ever recite poetry? Was there a playground? What did it look like? Was it in a field, or did it have pavement? Did it have swings? Did you ever fall out of one? Did you ever swing standing up? Was there a nurse to look after the children, or did the teacher doctor you? Who was the teacher's favorite? Who was your friend? What child did you like best? Whom didn't you like? Were you timid? Did your mother bring you to school? What did you have for breakfast? What was home like in the morning? Did your mother and father have breakfast with you? Can you remember wanting to get up for school, or did your mother have to call you many times? What did you do when it rained? Did you have a cat? A dog? (Patient productions about animals are usually gold mines!)

This line of questioning can be used for each school year, each session, each occasion, and so on. I have tried to give you an insight into the richness of this technique. I believe that, once started, only occasional proddings are necessary to keep the patient making these critical connections again and again. One factor, however, must be underscored, and this relates to the quality of your own interest. The success of this method will be directly proportional to the depth of your interest. If you are bored, forget it; it won't work. Nonetheless, you have to try anyway; it's the only way you'll discover how fruitful it can be.

Living Memories

To further demonstrate the value of this approach, I remind you of your own response when someone, obviously interested in you, asks you about a particular experience. "Oh!" you reply, "you visited Boulder Dam too this summer! You remember those huge rock formations around the base of the dam? And how about that dam! What did you feel when you stood there and looked up at that mass of concrete?" And you launch forth and spill every last association you have. You go on to tell of the marvelous meal you had in the little restaurant in the next town where the waiter's grandfather, who had been a buffalo hunter, was given a trophy for etc., etc., etc., etc. Isn't it all fun—and isn't it stimulating, exciting, satisfying, and endearing to engage in such exchanges when your listener is interested?

When do you think your patient last had an opportunity to feel this way, to talk this way, to experience unadulterated good or bad memories? Do you feel good talking about yourself in this way? How about giving him a chance to talk about himself in the same way? He needs it more than you—I hope! Give him at least the opportunity to try to experience it. He may not be able to go along with you, but you must try. Practice doesn't make perfect, but it helps a lot.

Perhaps your patient might say, "What's all this for? It isn't helping me. You're missing the boat." Don't be intimidated, if you really want to find out if it works. Or drop it and use it again another time. Remember, if that patient knew so well what was good for him, he would not be your patient. Maybe you don't know so much either, but you'll probably learn faster than he will, and you'll help him as you learn.

CHAPTER XII
Guilt Is a Feeling

Dead or Alive

"The only thing that makes me feel (human) is guilt!" a young woman outpatient told her therapist. She had been hospitalized subsequent to a suicide attempt. Following her discharge, she faithfully attended the sessions with her psychotherapist. She would constantly remark how "dead" she felt, how her feelings were "cut off"; she referred to herself as "not human." "I have no feelings... But if guilt is a feeling, then I'm more alive if I can feel it. You cannot take it away from me!"

These comments illuminate two points made previously. The patient's alienation from her feelings is clearly expressed when she speaks of lack of feeling and not being human. For her, then, the absence of feeling indicates a loss of humanness. How can one become reconciled to that? This young woman is nowhere near the question "Who am I?",which so many young people like to play with in these times. She is still with the *what*—"If I am not human, then *what* am I?"

The drama and the pathos inherent in her condition are further revealed when, stumbling across her response of guilt, she identifies it as a feeling. "Ah! I have come upon a feeling in myself. Well then, I must be human after all." Here we have a person clinging to her humanity. Can you understand that? Does anything in your experience help you to empathize with her? Will you permit her to keep that feeling or are you going to try to snatch it from her because it is not "good" to feel guilty?

But where have all the feelings gone, that the patient must cling to guilt to have any feelings at all? As the flowers, they were bombed away, burned away, repressed and depressed away. A good, pleasurable feeling is a delightful, sensitive, tender, fleeting entity for some. If a good feeling is crushed in the young, it becomes distorted, twisted beyond recognition, lost to the individual; or it may go underground and remain unavailable in its pristine, spontaneous, original form. It can be crushed by inattention, cruelty, harsh criticism, inappropriate discipline, indifference, overprotection, and other exaggerations.

Children are filled with natural, spontaneous feelings (as distinguished from those manufactured at a later age) of joy and sorrow, of happiness and sadness, of love and hatred, of confidence and fear. As some of them begin to feel that the world in which they live cannot accept their feelings when and in the way they are expressed, they learn to fear and distrust their own spontaneity; they come to believe that it can only result in difficulties and problems with parents, teachers, peers. In extreme cases, with psychic survival at stake, they are masters at learning how to "turn off" their feelings so as not to experience the intolerable anxiety resulting from conflict between their inner needs and the needs and demands they encounter in their immediate worlds.

A rich variety of solutions for feeling safe and acceptable are elaborated. Some learn to ride the crest of others' opinions and can only compulsively follow and appease: "Whatever you want to do is O.K. with me. I want it too." Others block out all but their own needs and desires. They believe implicitly that you are interested in only their welfare; they love you for loving them. These are the narcissists. Others learn to drive themselves toward perfectionistic goals known only to themselves, and all matters of life and all relationships are subjugated to those ideals. There are the ones who having been so hurt in early life, learn only to strike back indiscriminately at friend and foe alike, carrying on a relentless, lifelong crusade of vengeance. Another group leaves the field of action and learns to give solace to themselves with whatever resources that remain available. All compulsive solutions ultimately fail, for compulsiveness reduces autonomy to automaticity in its drive toward unrealizable goals.

Telling You

If we will but listen to our patients and credit them with a knowledge of certain things about themselves that is superior to our own, we can make some important discoveries about them. In this way, we may learn how to treat their illnesses more effectively. Treatment is best tailored to suit each patient. What works with one does not necessarily work with another.

One psychotherapeutic approach is to elicit from the patient *his* thoughts, *his* feelings, *his* needs, desires, wants, values, attitudes—not *ours*. Subsequent questions, based on data derived from our initial elicitations, help to recycle that data through the patient again. This helps him to better understand what he is saying, to come closer to it, and therefore closer to himself. In a sense, he needs the help of the therapist to sift through the data of his life. Much material is produced, and the therapist sifts out most of it, using only small nuggets of existence that exemplify either the patient's way of experiencing satisfaction, or his way of defending himself against a potentially hostile world. Only the patient can provide the needed data.

The young woman quoted above found her defense from suffering in keeping to herself. Having experienced only indifference and finally total abandonment in her early years, she learned her lesson well. Her solution was to become indifferent to life, and to survive her isolation by suppressing and denying any feelings which she felt could only cause her anguish. What is she saying to us? What is this business of feeling human only through guilt?

To Live, To Die

Basic requirements of existence include food, shelter, rest, and activity. Our intellectuality distinguishes us from animals, as does our complex emotionality. The latter includes an element of companionship and feelings toward self and others. Without these, persons who fulfill only physical requirements and function intellectually are some-times called computers—less than human—though, if their functioning is efficient and productive, they may be much admired.

The point being made here is that the experiencing of feelings is an essential aspect of humanness, without which too high a price is paid in terms of isolation and/or suffering. Experiencing is emphasized because all people have feelings all the time. But one can manage to keep from consciously experiencing feelings if one is fearful that they will be dis-turbing. In that event, the alienating process serves as a protective device. As long as it is not carried to an extreme, it is one way people can remain more comfortable with their anxieties. It can be stated also that unconscious defenses are aspects of and contribute to the alienating process.

Bereft of conscious feelings in their ordinary, everyday activity, people are as dead. Extremes are not often en-countered. But to the extent that the patient feels dead, he is being deprived in one way or another. There are those who can survive tolerably well, despite a sense of deadness, as long as they do not experience conflict. These persons rarely come to the attention of the psychotherapist. They live their lives out uneventfully in their own particular pursuits and are never conscious of the stench of their deadness. The gift of life and humanness has been theirs and they have never enjoyed it. If they ever realize that, they become furious with themselves and begin to thrash about, caught in a conflict between their living death and the fear and anxiety engendered by a wish to move into the world of life and consequent uncertainties. This might be called the "Princess Turandot syndrome." Her tortured writhings, when forced to the realization that she exists, but encased in ice, constitute the central theme of Puccini's last and perhaps greatest opera.

Alive Is Better

Whatever the cost, whatever the anguish, once baited with the feeling of aliveness, once aware, once wanting and needing, one cannot but attempt to search for more. The patient remains largely unconscious of what I am describing. Nevertheless, he may be driven into living because deadness is aberrant to life. Therefore, while any spark of aliveness is available to him, he will do anything, including the taking of self-destructive steps, to move toward it.

Without a sense of aliveness, one feels drained, hollow, disinterested, uninvolved, utterly bored. When such feelings break through to consciousness, they are unbearable. They are best tolerated only when they remain repressed or suppressed. Even then, they can be tolerated only poorly because feelings of deadness and emptiness are anxiety provoking also.

Anxiety cannot remain unbound indefinitely. There are two principal courses open—to seek psychotherapeutic help, or to engage in some activity which will serve to bind anxiety. Almost anything will serve, as long as it "works." Compulsive use of drugs, alcohol and sex are common pursuits for this purpose. Discovery of the alleviation of anxiety by such means is what confirms the compulsive character of those activities.

Compulsiveness

Here is the *raison d'être* of all compulsiveness, whatever its form. Any activity, thought, or feeling that relieves anxiety can become as an addiction—that is, a compulsion. The patient has neither awareness nor does he have the courage or strength to do without his compulsion; without it, he could experience anguish as great as that of any heroin withdrawal.

While destructive use of drugs, alcohol, and sex can be fairly easily understood as compulsive behavior, to which one may become addicted for the valid reason of relieving intolerable anxiety, other forms of compulsiveness often pass by unrecognized. Surely overworking, to the detriment of one's health and one's family relationships, is a form of compulsive behavior. Certain forms of telephone use, reading, TV viewing, gossiping, etc., are all around us and serve to fill unbearable hollowness and to relieve anxiety.

The test for compulsiveness can be made easily. When an individual feels that something he is doing is harmful, destructive, or interferes with his life goals, and he decides to eliminate it, yet finds that he is unable because anxiety levels rise to unwarranted heights, it can be said that he is caught in the grasp of compulsiveness, whatever form it takes. Thus, an unconscious decision has been made. Destructive though it may be, it is the lesser of two evils. "I can stand the destructiveness to my health and well-being better than I can stand the anxiety I'll feel if I give it up. So the choice is clear." Inability to stop smoking might be partially explained on this basis.

Referring to our patient above, if guilt is a feeling and is the only one available to her, then the patient is compelled to do what will make her feel guilty, so that she can feel *something*. Feeling nothing arouses devastating anxiety and she cannot stand that.

To Know Thyself

Let us examine the dynamics of certain phenomena that

we have observed over and over. We have heard many times that children, pupils, any of us, do things just to "get attention." That term is usually used to refer to youngsters or adults who do something disruptive, whether at home, in school, or anywhere. Lectures, scoldings, bribes, and promises seem to do no good. The recalcitrant child or adult often promises, militantly, that he will do better. Patients promise not to behave self-destructively. One is convinced of their good intentions. Yet, in a short period of time, here they are again with their disruptive behavior, followed by the inevitable cycle of accusation, guilt, remorse, recrimination; and promises start afresh and break down all over again. It might be assumed that no one likes to be disruptive, destructive, or incur disapproval. Approval is all, and we are all supposed to feel comfortable with it. So why does our patient, our child, or our friend repeatedly behave in a way that is almost guaranteed to incur our disapproval?

These phenomena might be better understood if we were to ask the following questions. What is your patient striving for? Is it a sense of affirmation for his very existence that is being sought? Does the child need approval so that he can establish his being in the world? If that is so, will anything do to confirm this, even disapproval? Admittedly, approval is preferable toward establishing a sense of self. But if it is not forthcoming, what is a child to do? What is our patient to do if he has never had this sense of affirmation? If he requires affirmation, in the form of approval, to take the next breath, and the approval is not forthcoming, he is as a drowning person who must take a breath to survive, but finds only water available. What happens then? He gasps, becomes panicky, he takes in anything around—and drowns. He can do no other.

Is there a parallel with the child from whom approval is withheld, whatever the reason? He must accept whatever is available to him—the next best or the next worst. If only disapproval is available, he uses that to confirm his existence in the world and thereby continues living. "I am the one disapproved of. Not great, but better than nothing!" As I said

earlier, psychic survival is at stake. Early in life, the
youngster can experience himself and know himself only
through his guardians' responses to him. If disapproval is all
that is available to him, so be it.

Here is a child or a patient, experiencing himself, his
sense of being, through the disapproval of his family, his
peers, his world. Involutions of the details are many. But
there it is. Once established for him, it is his means for survival. It is as if the drowning man miraculously discovered
that he could indeed survive the water. Then he would remain in it and, in doing so, become dependent upon it for
survival. It would, then, be difficult to persuade him to leave
it!

Once our patient discovers that there is a possibility for
psychic survival, spurious or otherwise, whatever the
means, he will seek them repeatedly and compulsively as
continuing insurance for survival. Let us assume that our
patient is having the following dialogue with himself.
(Actually, this dialogue is a composite of what patients have
said over and over, each in his own unique way.)

If disapproval is what I get and I can know who I am
through it, then if disapproval is withheld I must do something—anything— to incite my parent (spouse, therapist,
etc.) to give it to me. So I am disruptive, and my parents
get angry. That I know. I can see that clearly. It is unequivocal. I know who I am. I am that person who has
done this and who is receiving the brunt of the anger of
that person out there. That establishes me unequivocally
for this very moment. I have no doubts. I need feel no
anxiety, no sense of emptiness. I know who I am. I can be.
I may be a rotten kid, but at least I am that. It's better
than being nothing. Because then I would feel nothing. No
one would pay any attention to me. No one would see me
or notice me. I would become part of a room, part of the
landscape. I would become a thing. I could not stand that
barrenness, that limbo. It is far better that I am a hood, or
a drug user, or a dopey kid with long hair—anything, so

long as it identifies me in somebody's eyes—so long as I
can see and feel myself as *some* body rather than *no* body.
If I am a rotten kid and am punished, then I feel badly because I have caused pain to my parents, and I don't want
to cause them pain. Yet only when I cause them pain do I
get clear-cut, unequivocal, 100 percent responses. All the
other responses I get from them are confused, mixed up,
muddy. I never know exactly what they mean when they
talk with me. Are they telling me the truth when they say
something? They haven't been shown to be trustworthy in
the past. I get *double-messages* from them. When they
say yes, there seems to be a reluctance. I'm never sure if
they mean yes or no. And then the presents. What are
they for? Do they mean they like me, or do they want to
get me off their backs? The other kids get presents when
they do something their parents are proud of. I get them if
I'm bad or good. I don't know what they mean about anything anymore. And that tight expression on their faces
when they talk to me, when they say they love me. They
don't have to say that. I'll know it if they love me. But
that's funny. I don't think I do know it. Yet I don't know it
any better when they say they do. Most of the time when
they look at me, they seem angry. At best, they look sad.
It's sort of scary. No matter what they are saying, it
'smells' the same way. The look is angry, but sometimes
the content of the words is not. *I just don't know what
these words and looks mean any more.* But yelling,
beating, unadulterated anger I know. Give me that any
day. That's straight. That I can recognize. I know what's
going on then. I feel as though my feet are on the ground.
It's not as frightening as all the rest of the gobbledygook.
I am a bad person. That's what it says. That's what I am.
No ifs, ands, or buts about that. It establishes me—like
one, two, three—OK? It identifies me. There are no loose
ends. No mysteries. Then I feel bad (i.e., guilty) because
I've been a bad person in hurting them. I can feel this
guilt and it hurts me. At the same time, it makes me feel

good because it's straight. It's clear. It's clean. Maybe it sounds crazy—but it's like a breath of fresh air!

A flowing equation is another way of representing the above dialogue:

DISRUPTIVE BEHAVIOR ⟶ reaction of anger toward me ⟶ I am a bad person ⟶ hurts other ⟶ guilt in me ⟶ I'll try to do better ⟶ I do ⟶ other becomes indifferent ⟶ who am I now ⟶ am I dead or alive ⟶ panic ⟶ how can I find out if I'm dead or alive ⟶ I must do something to be noticed so I can know if I'm alive ⟶ DISRUPTIVE BEHAVIOR ⟶ reaction of anger ⟶ what a relief, now I know I exist again ⟶ but I've hurt the other ⟶ it's the only way I can get through to them that I'm here ⟶ I can't stand the indifference ⟶ it suffocates me ⟶ I drown. I must breathe to live ⟶ now they're responding ⟶ they feel angry ⟶ I feel guilty ⟶ now I can breathe ⟶ now I can live ⟶ I've jarred them from their indifference that makes me feel I'm lost in a whirlpool ⟶ oh, my guilt feels so good ⟶ it makes me feel alive. I can breathe ⟶ I won't let you take it from me. ⟶ that would be like letting you stab me ⟶ no, no, you can't take that away from me!

So Little

Is it possible that some patients, having developed in particularly convoluted ways because of early distorted family relationships, have to develop such a line of unconscious concern in order to achieve a sense of selfhood that most of us experience and take for granted in ourselves? Does that contribute anything to our understanding of their dilemmas? Does it force us to clarify meanings for the patient, as well as for ourselves, when we hear that a patient does not want us to take his feeling of guilt away? Can one be so impoverished with respect to feelings that he clings even to painful guilt feelings, requiring their own relief, and most probably leading to the development of other *neuroticisms?*

The patient answers, "I must be," to the query, "To be or not to be." Then he proceeds to be in any way that he can. What he has available to him may not be suitable, but if that's all there is, it will have to do. He is really quite resourceful. He has to make do with the feeling that *guilt is good*. Which one of us could turn that trick!

How To Treat

What can the tyro psychotherapist do, in terms of intervening into that compulsive pattern? I must repeat what has been said many times before, here and elsewhere. The cycle can be interrupted by our responses, which will be different from those our patient anticipates and from the way other people in his life have responded to his neurosis or psychosis. And if we do not respond in ways that give rise to guilt, then his need for feeling alive through guilt is not met. He may panic and feel that he is going to disappear. But wait. While we are not giving him the nourishment he craves and demands for maintaining life according to his posits (bad—anger—guilt—aliveness), we are nevertheless giving him sustenance. He does not recognize it, and he keeps on fighting for what he thinks he needs to survive. Yet he is not dying, even though he is not getting what he demands. "What is going on?" he asks.

We are feeding him "intravenously." He is being nourished but he doesn't know how. In a few days or weeks all he knows is that he's not dead. He was sure he would be if he couldn't continue as he was, even though he was not "making it." He keeps fighting, but not so ferociously. Do you remember that I said he needed affirmation? That is what he is getting from us now. Not affirmation in the form he is accustomed to, but affirmation nevertheless. We are affirming his existence by our unadulterated attentiveness. He has never had this kind before, because all the attentiveness he ever received, except certain forms of anger, was adulterated and, therefore, confusing to him.

Together with you, his therapist, he can traverse the road

from his hell, even if it's only for a limited time. You do not understand the intricacies of his illness. But can you observe, all eyes and all ears, as a compassionate human being listens to one who suffers, one who bears not one ounce of compassion for himself? You may feel pity for him. Don't be ashamed of that. Your pity, per se, won't help him, but it will help you to reach out to him. You may listen better if you feel pity. Feeling pity, you can do nothing to hurt him. Pitying him, you cannot feel impatience or anger toward him.

That doesn't mean that you become a "sucker" for his maneuverings. You still have your job to do. You still have to *conduct the therapy*. You still have to make appropriate decisions regarding management. These responsibilities do not preclude certain feelings on your part.

Essentially, I am saying that you provide your patient with a service by not becoming angry, impatient, or anxious. You will occasionally have such feelings anyway, even though they are of no use to your patient. To the extent, however, that you are free of them, you will afford your patient a new experience. I am saying that you can recognize your patient's suffering and can pity him. I am saying that your pity may help you to grasp his sense of bereftness and loneliness.

To do this is to begin to sense the pronounced need to enrich your impoverished patient's experience so that he may be able to relieve his emptiness. When you have some feeling for that, you have begun to know that you have the potential for this task. Once you believe that, you have taken a first step on the long journey of effective treatment for your patient. This journey is never completed, but that first step must be taken, sooner or later. Keep in mind the old Chinese proverb: *A thousand mile journey begins with but a single step.*

CHAPTER XIII
Who, What, Where, When, How, and Sometimes Why

Five and Sometimes Six

If I had to reduce psychotherapeutic technique for the beginner to elemental essentials, I would suggest the exclusive use of certain words. Like the vowels, there are five and sometimes six.

Use of these five or six words could (1) provide the uncertain novice with important data about his patient; (2) convey an interest in the details of the patient's life; (3) help the patient to make significant contact with what he is saying; (4) help to clarify for him things that have never been specifically pointed out before; (5) provide him with an opportunity to talk at length with someone other than an exasperated family and reluctant friends; (6) provide him with the chance to ventilate without fear of rejection or retaliation.

Furthermore, use of these few words would lessen the gratuitous (for the most part) "interpretations" that beginning therapists feel obliged to make, regardless of their relevance or the therapist's level of training or understanding of the dynamics of the patient's problems. I feel fairly certain that little would be lost, in terms of effective treatment, were inexperienced therapists advised to avoid making any interpretations beyond the most simple and obvious ones, until they were well into their own psychoanalytic training. Until such time, it is my opinion that the questions of *how, who, what, where, when, and* sometimes *why* would suffice.

133

The least useful of these is *why*. It is included here principally because you cannot resist using it. It doesn't matter how many times you may decide that it has not furthered your understanding of the patient's problems, you will use it anyway. It seems to be an intrinsic part of any interrogating process.

You ask the patient, "Why did you say that?" Very often, his reply is, "I don't know," or some variation of that. At times, the patient may reply, "If I knew I wouldn't be here." Sometimes he may say, in effect, "That's for you to know." Occasionally, he gives a seemingly logical reason, but it contributes little to further understanding. Often, he may offer a blatant rationalization, denial, or evidence of feelings of persecution. Those productions are not to be set aside, but to be dealt with as any other reply might be.

Whatever his reply, all too often the patient feels somehow "put down" by the question. In his mind, he interprets your simple question, "Why did you say (or do) that?" while you are merely seeking information, as "Why did you say (or do) such a dumb thing?" Certainly, oppositional patients, and indeed oppositional persons not in treatment, have a tendency to regard *any* question posed as some form of an adverse criticism. They are hypersensitive to the possibility of criticism and are incapable of dealing with it, real or imagined, in a rational manner.

It is true that upon occasion you may feel that your patient was imprudent. You want your patient to recognize this for himself in order to avoid possible future rejection and hurt. But the hypersensitive patient cannot appreciate this form of help and is flooded with feelings of unworthiness which derive from his own extensive self-critical tendency. Even when you have no intention of making such a point, the patient may very well externalize his own self-criticism upon you. He then deals with it by resistance, anger, and a sense of impotence. He rarely takes the easy way.

One goal for the tyro therapist is to help the patient to feel better about himself—that is, to improve his self-image. The question *why*, which may lead to an uncorking of self-denigration in the patient, is clearly not the most judicious of questions.

What is to be done? What questions can one ask that will lead the patient onto the pathway of discovery of inner strength? What questions will preclude further engagements with productions which may lead to further self-denigrating outcomes? Let us turn our attention now to the other five words—*who, how, what, where, when*. They are related to each other; they seek information without putting words into the patient's mouth and without making him feel cornered.

Five Cousins

Consider first what the purpose is of any questioning. Questions are asked for information leading to (1) an understanding of the patient's problems, (2) possible resolution or amelioration, and (3) improvement in the patient's status so that he can either leave the hospital, or, if not hospitalized, achieve a more comfortable state of being.

Keeping these purposes in mind, let us explore the use of the following simple questions. Your patient complains, "I had so many things I wanted to do over the weekend, and I didn't do a single solitary thing. I just can't seem to get started. What's the matter with me?" There he is again—at himself, and in a way that can only make him feel worse about himself. To answer, "You are so chronically depressed, isolated, and filled with self-hatred that you're doing great if you just got yourself something to eat over the weekend," is not useful. Rather:

"*What* was it you wanted to do?"
"Oh, I don't know. Lots of things."
"*What* things?"
"My clothes were all dirty and I had nothing left to wear."
"*How* do you clean them?"
"I have to take them to the laundromat."

"*Where* is that?"

"About six blocks away."

"*How* do you get there?"

"That's the trouble. I either have to walk or take a bus."

"*How* do you manage your bundle of laundry?"

"Not very well. It's heavy. And I don't like to traipse through the streets with it."

"Does that have anything to do with your trouble getting started?"

"No it doesn't. But I hate to carry it through the streets."

The last question is an interpretive one, suggesting that there is a reason for the patient's not being able to get started on the weekend—in this case, with his laundry. An immediate denial follows: "No, it doesn't." Yet his next words are consonant with the interpretation: "I hate to carry it through the streets." Perhaps the bundle is too heavy. More likely, however, is the fact that he hates it because the idea of carrying laundry through the streets doesn't quite jibe with the image he tries to maintain for himself. That image certainly does not include being his own laundry boy!

Neurotic Pride

An image many young men hold in common is related to some form of "machismo," in one or more of its infinite variations. Feelings of humiliation derive from unfulfilled grandiosity needs (pride) of that image. In order to maintain whatever image he has elaborated for himself through the years, your patient subjects himself to the tortures of immobilization and isolation rather than go out and be a "laundry boy." In his imagination, that is something he feels he could tolerate even less than his other devils. In most cases, that would not be so; physical mobilization, together with possible contact with another person, as well as some small sense of accomplishment might possibly yield him more comfort than any fantasy of being too far above that.

There is no point, however, in trying to uncover these dynamics with your patient, for it cannot be clear yet what should be done with them, once uncovered. The sole necessity is to relieve the patient of his shame and sense of guilt regarding his inability to get a simple thing like laundry done. Such relief is the therapeutic effect for which we are striving at this point. Even though his denial is emphatic, your patient now has a valid reason for not getting "started." That is better than having no reason at all, to see himself only as a "good-for-nothing slob," who can't even provide himself with clean clothing! Finding that reason is perhaps only the lesser of two evils. But under the circumstances, we are grateful for small results.

As your patient has such encounters with you, and if he is relieved even in a small way, he begins to associate you with a state of diminished suffering. He begins to look to you as his therapist and will be more willing to cooperate in therapy. Your questions have not proven threatening to him. When you made your interpretation with a question, he defended himself immediately with a denial. Yet he is relieved. Therapeusis is proceeding.

Softly, Softly

To continue a dialogue with your patient, you might ask: "*What* else did you expect to get done this weekend?"; "*When* did you expect to do those things?"; "*How* were they to be done?"; "*Who* was to help you?"; and so on. Of course, the questions selected depend upon context. Your patient's answers to the question *how* may serve to inform both patient and therapist that expectations were unrealistic for accomplishing the task under discussion. For the therapist to imply, in effect, "Well, you know, your expectations aren't very realistic, so you shouldn't feel inadequate," makes the patient feel yet more inadequate, for he immediately feels he should have known they were not realistic. He can argue that the expectations are reasonable, only his ineptness causes failure. With your questions, we hope that your patient will himself discover that he could not do *this* thing if he were busy doing *that* thing at the same time. He has a sense of accomplishment when he reaches this point. He is not usually aware that you have led him there with your *hows, whos, whats, wheres, whens.* But again, you can share his discovery with him by continuing to keep your words to a minimum.

This approach may not work with some patients. But it works well with patients who talk easily. Since a majority of patients are willing to talk, an approach using these questions can be easily tested. If you find it of no help, it can be discarded. However, you might be surprised at what you uncover when your patient follows your gentle lead with your innocuous questions as, "What did you say?"; "What did he say?"; "What did you do then?"; "Who said that?"; "What kind of expression did he have?"; "What was his tone of voice?"; "How did you feel at that time?"; "When did you think that?"; "Where were you when he said that?"; and "How did you react to what he said?"

There is hardly anything which the patient says that cannot be further elucidated by such questioning. I suggest that you try this approach for a few sessions to test it. If you try it, you may like it.

CHAPTER XIV
Notes on Feelings

Good Is Out Too

In simplistic terms, feelings are good, bad, or nonexistent. Absence of feeling usually indicates some measure of repression or suppression. Because good feelings are pleasurable, one may assume that repressed feelings are bad or painful, and that the patient is obliged to exclude them from consciousness to avoid pain. He does not intend, however, to relegate good feelings to the realm of nonexistence. Unfortunately, at times the "baby is thrown out with the bath water." That is, good feelings, as well as bad, are liquidated.

The rationale for that is based upon avoidance of all feelings. After all, one cannot predict positive or negative outcomes. Therefore, to preclude possible hurts, all feelings must be avoided as much as possible. You've all heard, "Ah yes, I was burned once. I'll never love anyone again. It was too painful when we broke up." Ah yes, it may very well have been, especially if one's pride was damaged. But think of all the fun and joy that's missed when one avoids loving in the first place. In extreme cases, success in avoidance of feelings of any nature, may leave the patient *a-feeling*, or in clinical terms, with a flat affect.

That may be what has happened to your patient who says he has no feeling about anything. He has successfully (in his terms) squelched his awareness of feelings that arise in response to severely stressful interpersonal or intrapsychic stimuli.

While intending to deal only with so-called bad feelings in this way, however, he ends up suppressing many other responses. The vigilance required to keep feelings from consciousness keeps the patient in a tense state, with anxiety constantly flowing. Busy with this "police work" against possible hurt, your patient cannot recognize or be receptive to stimuli which might lead him to harbor good feelings. All is suspect.

Even if common sense indicates that someone is reaching out warmly to him, he finds "explanations" (rationalizations): "He is doing that because he wants something from me"; "He sounds friendly, but he must have something up his sleeve"; "If he really likes me, then he's stupid because I'm not worth liking. And if he's so stupid, I can't trust him or have anything to do with him"; and so on and on it goes.

Whatever his course, the result is the same. He succeeds in eliminating most feelings from consciousness and, in doing so, reduces the opportunity to respond to warm overtures. But I repeat—his intention is to deaden or to eliminate only the painful. He is not aware of his frequently total exclusion of the merry, the humorous, the playful, and the loving.

Low Key: Choice or Compulsion

This deadening of feeling has been a frequent finding in psychiatric patients. In recent years, however, a pattern of flatness has become common in the general population. In a sense, it seems to have been cultivated by certain people, so that they would "come on" as very "low key" or as "cool." Low keyness is not flatness, however, as long as it remains *choiceful*. But if it becomes choiceless—that is, compulsive—it pervades the entire personality indiscriminately. When any attitude or form of behavior becomes choiceless and indiscriminate, it moves into the realm of neurotic defensiveness against expected attacks. While we do not go about saying that thousands of people have a flat affect, it is my opinion that the dynamics of compulsive forms of so-called coolness are similar to those which result in the evolution of flat affect in the psychiatric patient.

Your patient does succeed to some extent in shutting off painful feelings. But the degree to which he succeeds only announces the beginning of a greater failure; for the price of his success is a robot-like existence—the ultimate failure of humanness. With increased suffering resulting from a state of alive/deadness, a condition too frequently without parallel, bad feelings may seem more desirable than no feelings at all. Parenthetically, I want to say that one of the reasons for the popularity of violence in its many forms may very well be the desire of the alive/dead to experience more aliveness through the jarring impact of violence.

Alive/Dead

A distinction must be made here between the alive/deadness of nonpatients and patients. Nonpatients who suffer from alive/deadness (or dead/living) are more successful, in that they do not feel the pressure, as do our patients. They have so ordered and regulated their lives that they become well insulated to the ravages of an alive/dead state. Belief in their own success is implicit; suffering is at a minimum. Alienation from their feelings is effective in protecting them from acute pain. They provide themselves with a kind of solid, impermeable armor. Such a person has little incentive to seek treatment. In his view, he is "doing fine." Only when the shield of alienation is broken through, does he experience deep suffering. In other words, only if hurt feelings escape the barrier of alienation, (the entire sum of one's defenses), will one feel sufficiently distressed to seek relief in treatment.

This means that the person who complains of alive/deadness has been unsuccessful at burying his distress, because he is actually struggling for aliveness. Somehow, something has pushed its way through. Once he has incidentally and accidentally experienced out-reaching warm feelings, he is thrown into conflict. He cannot deny them to himself, and despite the possibility of pain, any feeling is preferable to nonfeeling (a-feeling).

Feeling vs. A-feeling

It is at this stage that we often find our patients. They are struggling to emerge and cannot. On the one hand, they do not want to deaden themselves by squeezing themselves into constricted areas of existence. Yet, the anxiety generated by a wish to break away from deadness is too great. They feel trapped, fragmented, confused, disoriented. Even delusions and hallucinations may result as they attempt to make some order out of a terrible sense of disintegration. This rended apart feeling is caused by conflict—by the wish to leave a state of alive/deadness and the wish to remain with it in order to ensure safety.

The war one wages, however, is too much. Refuge is sought in some form of treatment where all will be taken care of and put right. In one sense, hospitalization may serve as a recessive factor. Removing the patient from the field of battle (conflict) denies him the opportunity to "slug it out" with himself. But frequently he is too weak to fight alone, and there is no alternative. In that case, it would be an un-kindness to deny him the safety of an institution.

The hospitalized patient is permitted an opportunity to engage in his struggle to survive in a less a-feeling way. For the most part, like the obstetrician, the psychotherapist serves as deliverer of whatever new life the patient is capable of claiming for himself.

When the patient experiences and lays claim to "bad" feelings—"I want to feel my guilt. Don't take it away from me!"—he might be on the threshold of emergence from deadness, from a-feeling. He will no longer settle for that;

he can no longer settle for it. Actual death sometimes seems preferable. This person can become the suicide patient, strongly motivated to seek an out, even though his solution may turn out to be his destruction. After a failed attempt, however, and with your help, he may be able to succeed in changing his search to a less deadly one. He is well primed for a change in attitude. His attempt attests to that wish.

Help!

The patient who makes a suicide *gesture* is also strongly motivated. Because he uses (consciously or unconsciously) a method with a built-in failure component, he places himself in a position where he can be helped, knowing that such a move is not likely to go unnoticed.

A patient's suffering finally drives him not directly into treatment, perhaps, but at least to your notice. We must remember that however he seems to try to defeat you, he is desperate for your services. Can you permit yourself to see him primarily as a sufferer, hungering for your help, rather than as the resisting, maneuvering schemer? Remember that for the most part he has dealt with pathology in his own family. Can you provide him with something different, something less contrived, less anxiety producing? Is the fear of being defeated in our minds or in his? Is he out to defeat *us?* Or is he just being himself in the only way he knows? Defeating, yes, certainly to himself and to those who have shared in the evolution of his illness.

Who Loses What

But how can we be defeated if we do not enter a contest where someone must lose? Our work together concerns *his* struggle to live. Can we somehow convey to him that one neither wins nor loses in that work, but that one learns to be?

True, you are in the line of fire. But aren't you better equipped against being grievously wounded and defeated?

We can be defeated only if, losing our position, we permit defeat to enter into our own hearts and minds. Except in physical terms, all defeat is self-inflicted. This may seem high sounding, but consider the statement for a moment. If you can believe that your patient is being himself and not busy testing *you*, resisting *you*, defeating *you*, your entire presence with him will be on another plane.

If you are primarily worried about being defeated, letting him have the "upper hand," you can become anxious and may be distracted from your task. That task is to help your patient to feel that you are there with him, right in on his field of battle—not fighting the battle for him (you cannot anyway) but supporting him in every way that you can, responsibly, and giving him sustenance every step of the way. Your questions, your comments are all part of this support: "How did that feel?"; "What did you do next?"; "Do you think about that very much?"; "How does that trouble you?"; "I don't understand that. Will you clarify it?"; etc., etc. There are many words and facial expressions that can say, "I am here with you at your shoulder as you struggle. Should you fall or be wounded, if you permit it, I'll be there to help you to reenter your struggle."

Questions cannot be labeled as right or wrong. They are better described as productive or nonproductive. This is one reason why supervisors often seem to dissent among themselves. Each has his own brand of question or comment. At times, some words seem to be more useful than others. But I suspect that the usefulness of any of them depends upon their employment as an unqualified, continuous message of assistance.

In that position, there can be little concern with defeat, with being maneuvered, with being the victim of sadistic behavior. All of those positions require two activators—the perpetrator and the victim. The therapist must assume responsibility for his position, sooner or later. If he does not want to place himself in a particular position, he has only to choose not to. Without a victim, there can be no defeat;

without a subject, no one can dictate. When we feel vanquished by our patient, we can raise the question: In what way did we choose our defeat?

Mixed Feelings

Instead of good or bad, we might label feelings as pleasant or unpleasant. Single-faceted feelings lend themselves to such simple labeling. But multi-faceted feelings may contain elements of contradiction making them more difficult to identify. When a person says, "I have mixed feelings about that," he is usually referring to contradictory elements. In our patients, contradictions are usually due to unconscious conflicts which keep an iron grip on the patient, precluding his involvement in pursuits which might be conducive to a sense of well-being.

In working with a patient who is talking about feelings of neglect, the following may be considered. Does he feel neglected in a diffuse, vague way, or does he actually believe that he is being neglected by someone out there, one who is actively neglecting him? If that is his belief, is it a feeling? If it is not a feeling, then what is he feeling while he is believing that he is being neglected by someone or everyone? Does he feel anger that he should be so abused, that anyone should be doing this to his august person? Is his feeling one of loneliness? Is it one of sadness that there seems to be no recourse open to him? Is it sadness, rooted in a belief that the possibility for experiencing any joy is dead, if indeed it ever existed at all? "Yes, it did," your patient says. "Once, as a child, when we went to Uncle Jack's for the holidays, I felt so good, so happy, so alive. I can never forget that feeling." But it is no more and never can be, he feels. He is sad at the hopelessness of never recapturing the feeling again. He describes it like feeling sad when someone has died. It's a loss, an irretrievable loss and he cannot get over it, nor can he do anything about it. He believes in his impotence, and grows angry with himself.

Attempts to clarify one's feeling often lead to the uncovering of multiple feelings. The patient complains, "I am feeling frustrated." "What is frustration for you?" asks the therapist. It turns out to be varying quantities of anger, impatience, helplessness, disappointment, discouragement, even hatred. Is the frustration a feeling, or is anger the feeling? Again the question: does your patient believe he is being frustrated by an imaginary or a real entity out there and feels very angry about it and wants to eliminate a particular person or institution? If it is a feeling, it is surely a complex one.

Demands

What does your patient mean when he says that he feels abused by his parent, his spouse, or his offspring? Does this mean that he feels angry that the other does not relate to him as he wishes? Your patient continues, "He goes his own way. He does not fulfill my needs and expectations. He isn't even aware of them. He only imposes his wishes upon me which I must accede to if I do not want to be abandoned. I cannot because I feel (believe) I am too dependent and I might die. So I have to meet his needs for no one sees to mine. I feel so neglected and abused. I could die of frustration!"

Which are the feelings here? Are there only feelings of anger and rage? Are all the other complications that cause the feeling of pain actually beliefs, demands, expectations, in addition to those of fear and anger?

Which Questions

When the therapist asks his patient, "What do you think or feel?" he has to be prepared for a wide range of possible responses. Depending upon his objective, he will pursue one or another course in the therapeutic session. Some young workers believe that patients should be asked only how they feel about something and not what they think about it. Yet both are useful, for the patient may not make any distinction between them. How different a response would you elicit were you to ask, "How do you feel about the Jets?" or "What do you think about the Jets?"; "What do you feel about your mother-in-law?" or "What do you think about your mother-in-law?" While these questions are clearly different ones, they could be answered the same way, depending upon the feeling involved.

If one were to ask you what you felt about this administration, you might answer "rotten" or "great." But if asked what you thought about the administration, you might answer that you thought it could take such and such a position, or that it was doing well under the circumstances—about which you feel good or bad. There are many distinctions to be made. But our patients often cannot make them, for they are not clear about what they think or feel. The therapist may, then, try it all ways. If "What do you feel?" elicits no response, one asks, "What do you think?" Once the patient produces something, you have a beginning toward further investigation.

If you are curious and can depart from your preconceptions, you will discover a great deal about your patient's inner life. As he talks and feels your presence next to him, his hurt is being partially healed. Your continuing interest, acceptance, and care are as granulation tissue to the deep wounds that brought him into treatment. At your stage of development, you cannot prevent future wounds. The best you can do is help him to heal some facets of what he brings you. Helping the patient develop a more effective immunological system, so that he becomes less susceptible to the ravages of his disease, is the task of long-term treatment.

CHAPTER XV

Beginnings of Violence

Forms

Most psychotherapists are only occasionally obliged to treat violence in their patients. In an institution, the therapist has an entire staff to assist him if necessary. While the treatment of violence will not be the focus in this chapter, I want to include these remarks for whatever they may add to the beginner's understanding of violence.

Many questions invariably arise in any discussion on violence. Are people becoming more personally violent because there is so much violence about them? Are they becoming callous because so many others seem to be callous? Or does exposure to violence help to preclude a movement in that direction? Does the barrage of negative qualities of certain aspects of life through the various media infect people? Over a period of time, does this barrage of often sickening events serve to corrupt and coarsen the mind?

As commonly used, the term *violence* refers to the use of force with destructive intent. This form is always obvious and includes warfare, bombings, and murder, at one extreme, and street or family brawls, at the other. However, violence would also seem to include language forms, filled with fury and passion, designed to be destructive. Such forms are evoked during political campaigns by some politicians whose goal is the annihilation of the strengths of the opponent's position or of his reputation. Such forms are implicit also in extreme forms of malicious gossip and among some family members whose verbal exchanges seem to be dedicated to the decimation of the partner's or child's regard for himself.

Concepts of violence may also be associated with feelings that give rise to thoughts of annihilation regarding another. Many children, at one time or another, have been so enraged by a parent as to wish for his death. Some have actually thought of killing a parent, following a particularly strong provocation, perhaps some act of parental cruelty. While there is a vast difference between the thought and the deed, one may assume that a violent feeling or thought must precede the actual deed. Homicide among family members is not uncommon.

Are less explicit forms of violence those which arouse most concern? Probably not, even though it is necessary to understand the motivations of these forms in order to better understand more explicit forms. For the most part, when one speaks of violence, he probably is considering overt, destructive acts. However, a final destructive act of violence can be considered only as *one* possible outcome of a constellation of feelings.

Virtually every person has the ability to be violent and also the capacity to decide whether or not he will be violent. Where this capacity to decide seems to be inoperative, one can only assume that some form of compulsiveness has made it impossible for the individual to retain a freedom of choice in this matter.

There are events, caused by external stimuli, which could lead an ordinary nonviolent person to decide to resort to violence. Examples of this might be necessary homicide in order to protect one's self or one's family from death, or a starving animal-lover who must kill an animal in order to survive, or a kidnapped diplomat who must use physical force against his captor in order to escape, or a bystander who is physically assaulted and must defend himself. This kind of response has a quality of immediacy and may be viewed as appropriate to the stimulus. It is usually short-lived and does not continue past the point of essential effectiveness.

Inner Violence

More common, however, is the use of violence which has its roots in a quality of inner or private violence. This may or may not require external stimulation for its activation. One of the characteristics of private violence is that it is indiscriminate and may suddenly erupt in circumstances which, from a rational point of view, should not elicit a violent reaction. The evolution of this kind of behavior is the outcome of one's development in the context of one's family and immediate environment. It is a violence which often finds expression in adulthood through verbal abuse, sarcasm, contempt, consistently biting humor; through fantasies of destruction; or by means of spectator satisfactions.

Understanding an individual's private violence requires an exploration of his beginnings, where one will find an environmental matrix of anxiety, tension, and rejection. This matrix may nourish a child's propensity to develop not only in the direction of violence, but also in the direction of any form of aberrant behavior which diminishes the possibility of realizing his human potential and achieving a sense of well-being.

The child who is made fearful and anxious by family tensions, including violence, may respond with violence or some form of lesser or watered down aggressiveness. He may also respond with withdrawal, in the hope that he will not elicit any further violence, and that, if it erupts, he will not be noticed. This stance of withdrawal, however, is selected (unconsciously) by the child mainly because he has discovered somehow that he can bind, or allay, his anxious feelings in this way, and so make life more tolerable for himself. The child may respond in yet another way to family tensions. He becomes excessively compliant in the hope of warding off any possible damage to his psychic as well as his physical growth. By being regarded as a "good child," he hopes to avoid being subjected to violence.

Moves against (aggression), away from (withdrawal), or toward (compliance), or any combination of them, are the major moves any person might make in his particular world. The healthy person generally has the choice of selecting one or the other on the basis of appropriateness. Having developed particular maneuverings which he regards as safety measures for ensuring his survival, an anxiety-ridden child tends to respond with those maneuverings, whether or not they are indicated in the particular situation in which he may find himself. For example, if the child responds to an approach of affection with hostile aggression or withdrawal even though he needs and wants the affection, the other person can be repulsed and will withdraw his affection, leaving the child bereft. The youngster's inability to respond with warmth to affection points to his rootedness in a compulsive form of behavior. This compulsiveness is measured by his propensity to repeat patterns which clearly serve only to distance him from others.

While such patterns do not always interfere with a child's functioning, he generally will not be able to perform satisfactorily either for himself or for others; he may not be able to learn or be taught, participate or enjoy, or be spontaneous. To be spontaneous is to relinquish, upon occasion, one's guard. The need to be consistently on guard interferes with one's performance. The anxious youngster may manifest such a need in either academic or social spheres. He often feels ashamed of his poor performance and cannot realize that it rests upon a base of fear, conflict, and anxiety, all of which produce continuous distractions in his efforts to grow and develop. He therefore concludes, consciously or otherwise, that he must indeed be an inept, incompetent, inadequate, and, therefore, worthless person. His family may be feeding into these feelings continuously by their remarks about his shortcomings. Even though such remarks may be made jocularly, they often serve to confirm the youngster's bad feelings about himself.

Circular System

Because of guilt feelings the privately violent individual may have struggled for a long time to restrain and control his inner thoughts and impulses toward violence. However, in the past few years he may have experienced a sense of release. There are sociological and psychological factors responsible for this. Among them, may be more generally humane responses to violence. The privately violent individual may regard his rationalizations and denials as more valid and therefore feel less guilt-ridden. His secret feelings or acts of violence may then surface in a group, and his actions may impel an entire group to act with him. The movement of the group encourages him further, and a snowballing process is initiated. This process can also be viewed as a circular system, or as a two-way street between an individual and his peers, through which violence imperils each side with its contaminating power.

A circular system also is in operation within the individual, between what he feels to be his strengths and a profound sense of helplessness. This system seems to prevail in every case of violence, whether in an individual or in a group. The sense of helplessness derives from a failure to gain something to which the violator feels entitled. Whether or not his wish is justified is immaterial. Regardless of the real circumstances, the violator takes the failure as a personal one.

Pride may keep feelings of inadequacy from being stirred sufficiently to cause grief. But when its façade-like quality fails, the individual is left confronting that which he has attempted to keep hidden with the façade. Rage, both at his fallen pride and at being exposed, renders him impotent in the confrontation. Incapable of examining this painful humiliation, either for verification or for obsolescence, he attempts to get rid of the confrontation as quickly as possible and to vindicate himself in the process. Logic, for him, dictates that damaged pride will be restored by a pursuit of the "glory road," the attainment of which will once more reveal him to be all powerful in his own imagination, if nowhere else. If violence is the way to this goal, then that is the choice made. Deliberate violence is designed to gratify a wish immediately. If successful, it restores the violator's sense of rightness; and a repaired façade (pride) provides him with a kind of hollow authenticity.

A few common examples will illustrate this hopelessly circular system. A mother, feeling helpless and losing all sense of her capacity to deal with her recalcitrant child, strikes him in order to insure his obedience, thereby restoring her opinion of herself as an effective parent. Unfortunately, this solves nothing because her rage at her helplessness in the first place, and her guilt, act to incapacitate her once again. The child who feels helpless to elicit the friendship of his peers resorts to bullying others in order to instill fear and a spurious respect. The law-enforcing agent, feeling himself belittled and undermined, strikes out to restore his sense of power, without which he may feel he has no function, no reason for being.

An impetus toward violence, especially collective violence, can also be noted in offensive warfare. Though an individual can see the utter absurdity of killing another individual who is a complete stranger to him, large groups of people can be propelled into mass takings of life. In arousing a move toward collective violence, a strong appeal is made to a pride in the maintenance of an image of one's self as the strong one, the lover of liberty, the protector of the weak, and so forth. While one can feel strong and love liberty without gun in hand, the professional soldier does not afford himself the luxury of such a position. For him, to fight is to be strong and courageous, and not to fight is to be weak and cowardly. This view makes it almost impossible for the soldier to place himself in the latter position because of the weight of custom and tradition, and because of the regard of his comrades. Using the principle of circularity, one can see how this notion permits him to disclaim a poor view of self and to perpetuate a view of strength and power. According to that principle, an impetus toward violence may be regarded as an avoidance of a view of self which would be intolerable, and as utilization of an opportunity to overcome a basic sense of impotence.

To the extent, therefore, that the privately violent individual cannot learn to live with or to examine his failures, he will be driven to violence by an inner intolerance of those failures. Alone, he may not be able to give expression to his drive, and his violence remains private. If he feels aided and abetted, however, in some real or fancied way, by public attitude and behavior, he may be encouraged to act.

In this way, the lonely, detached assassin is driven, by his distorted interpretation of social change or of personal injury, to feel justified in asserting his rights by action. The potential for violence, which has its beginnings in early family experiences, is released in him and translated into explosive action. The more important the person assassinated, the more justified and glorified the violator's existence becomes. Whatever the consequences, surely he can never again regard himself as an inconsequential person, worthy only of disrespect.

Life-Feeling

In Chapter XII, I discussed feelings of nothingness and how anxiety-producing they are. Sometimes the victim will do anything, including suicide and murder, to overcome them. We have all heard of the so-called senseless murders, where fragmented, decompensated persons, at the bottom of the feeling scale, committed a murder "just for kicks." What they are saying is that, being presented with an opportunity to *feel*—to be human, if only for a moment—they could not resist it. What a way to feel human!

But the opportunity to feel excitement, quickened respiration and heartbeat, delivering a spurt of life through a cold, deadened spirit is not to be turned from. And in these times, with distorted and complex aftermaths of such acts, not only does this person get a momentary infusion of life-feeling from his act, but he also benefits from a prolonged life-feeling in the *acclaim* he receives for his act. If his act is sufficiently dastardly, he will receive instant notoriety (sometimes worldwide). In some instances, his pitifully impoverished "memoirs" become precious. And in some cases, he even makes it into the encyclopedia!

That's quite a leap from nothingness. His entire life shifts; his crime provides him with an organizing principle for his existence. Coming from an abysmal void, he now moves with purpose, direction, and a strong, unmistakable identity. His "life style," past, present, and future, becomes news-worthy. Instant fame is his. All dreams of glory are fulfilled. What has it cost him? If he was nothing, if he had nothing, it can cost him nothing. What does it give him? Everything! Are you still with me? Is this crazy? Of course. But what else are we talking about here?

Family Influences

As was mentioned above, a recourse to violence is only one possible outcome of a constellation of feelings. Such an outcome derives from very early and continous interpersonal and intrapsychic experiences. The quality of parental atti-tudes both between themselves and toward the child will de-termine, to a large extent, the child's degree of health. For example, where the parents are self-critical, and critical and rejecting of each other, the likelihood is that they will have, in some ways, critical and rejecting attitudes toward the child.

While intending to be good parents, they are limited in their ability to establish for the child a sense of peace and comfort or a sense of being cared for unconditionally, with-

out having to fulfill certain expectations. Most parents cannot help having some of these expectations. Nevertheless,
where parental demands are not intense, and where there
are many opportunities for the child to feel cared for, he does
not have to concern himself with intrapsychic elaboration of
façades designed to make himself interpersonally
acceptable.

Where parents are unaware of their demands but are consistent in expressions of dissatisfaction, the child begins to
feel at fault. He cannot regard his parents' unfortunate attitude toward each other and toward him as something apart
from him. The small child's natural egocentricity does not
permit such differentiation. He begins the arduous task of
trying to become a child who is desirable, but never
succeeds, because such parents cannot be satisfied. If he
cannot feel acceptable, then he assumes that he must be unacceptable, and eventually feels that his unacceptability is
based upon some fault within himself.

He surmises that he must be a terrible person, a stupid
person, an ugly one, a despicable one. It is difficult to name
all of the unhappy, imagined self-images which may be at
the heart of every neurotic development. Even when he is
with persons who care for him unqualifiedly, his response is
still influenced by the unintentionally rejecting parents, and
he ends up rejecting himself as well. This is the origin of the
basic worthlessness previously mentioned. Such an
individual, therefore, cannot believe that caring persons
really like *him* as he is with all of his "unacceptableness."
He can only assume that they seem to like him because he
has managed to cover up what is so "bad" in himself. As he
grows older, he often develops an unconscious contempt for
caring persons because they are so easily fooled by his
façades into believing that he is really a fine fellow. He
"knows" that he is not and he may feel contempt because
they care for such a despicable fellow. If this is so, he
reasons, then they are stupid, and therefore, not worth very
much themselves; and he will have no part of them.

All the while, however, this is running counter to a simultaneous and crying need for companionship and human affection which he constantly seeks. These opposing moves become compulsive, and it is a sorry conflict into which he is driven. The rending power of this conflict, in later years, may contribute toward a susceptibility to forces which influence him to commit violence in one form or another.

One of the factors basic to an act of violence is imitation. The child, who is reared in a family which used violence for resolving either anxiety or family conflicts and who is susceptible to feelings of emptiness and anxiety, may very well select the course of violence in resolving his conflicts as an adult. Hendin described some of his patients as coming "alive only through acts or fantasies of violence. Merely talking of past fights or brutality made them far more animated than usual."

Upon his early development, then, will rest each person's propensity for violence, whether of individual, private, or collective variety. Even though social and economic forces exert considerable influence upon parental attitudes also, it cannot be doubted that the immediate family influences upon a child are primary shaping forces, and as such influence his entire existence.

Parental impact may not be felt actively by an individual until he is an adult. Experiences as an infant and child are results of interactions with parents. The concern of a young person is whether parental attitudes make him feel that he is "all right" or "not all right" in their eyes. To the extent that he can grow with the feeling that all is well between himself and his family and world, feelings of frustration, fear, and emptiness will be minimal.

Collective Violence

There seems to be no one type of person who engages in public or collective violence. There are the instigators, the followers, and the indifferent ones. The instigator is often an active, assertive person for whom violence may be one way of life. He is probably the most likely to initiate acts of public violence. The follower is one who likes to please for whatever sense of security it affords him. Left to his own devices, the follower may not initiate overt violence, but he can be easily influenced to become a joiner. The indifferent person is perhaps one who feels most hopeless and most removed from a sense of personal involvement. He may, however, be infected by the excitement and mobilizing force of violence, as well as by the appeal of its attendant cause. If his indifference and passivity can be overcome, he may become the one most dedicated to the use of violence.

Another matrix in which violence finds its origins is in the impact of political and social attitudes of parents or other significant adults. Older children and young adolescents are particularly adept at soaking up such attitudes, whether or not the adults intend that they should. Because of limited experience and general ignorance, youngster's impressions are often riddled with inaccuracies and distortions. Adults, however, seem to be unaware of distorted impressions received by some youngsters, especially in cases where an adult is convinced of the rightness of his position and assumes that everyone else understands it. That phenomenon is observed again and again in clinical practice where there is the opportunity to speak with both the parent and the child individually or together. Words uttered by a parent may or may not be the words heard by the child. Even if the words spoken and heard are the same, the meanings assigned to them may be widely discrepant. Neither party, however, is aware of the discrepancies of understanding; and each may be quite shocked when he comes upon the fact of the discrepancy.

An unequivocal position, not necessarily being imposed upon a youngster, but to which he is exposed, is more influential than one might suppose. That is because a youngster has a natural tendency to identify with significant adults. Furthermore, the child often has no position of his own, and it gives him something of a feeling of importance to have one, even though it is borrowed.

Dynamically, this can be explained on the basis of his lack of a sense of self. A borrowed position makes him feel more substantial in that respect. At the same time, inaccuracies and distortions can result from a tendency of the young person to swallow the whole bit without discrimination, without weighing various parts, something the adult has long since learned to do. The youngster has no choice in what he hears and inadvertently learns in the home. Frequently, no one bothers to find out if he is learning what he hears the way it is intended to sound.

Perhaps this description is oversimplified, but it is important to recognize the literal quality found in some young people. That quality may exist either because of their inexperience or because they possess a normal gullibility together with an untarnished trust. Distorted impressions may lead later to unforeseen, destructive repercussions in which rabid justifications are found for blatant acts of lawlessness. Such an outcome of subtle or obvious influences leads one to postulate that many a young person is trapped with the license, but without the wisdom, for free action.

Social Expressions

That is especially evident in some school children when one group of adults wishes to gain control over a school—and move in against the established system in an angry, violent fashion. For these youngsters, adults have helped to bring a sense of violence right into the school building, spearheaded by an undisputed intention of improving conditions for the children. In so doing, however, the child's domain is being invaded, where traditionally, he has had to deal only with teachers and peers. But now, the child is infected with the virulent anger, the impatience, the resentment of the adult, and he has almost no resources to deal with this in a constructive manner. He feels insecure and restless; the faculty becomes more tense; classrooms become "grim and joyless." Such a situation is not only antithetical to that which parents and community are seeking, but the child is given new prototypes with which to identify.

While violence breeds violence, the child's use of it in the school cannot have the same grounding as that of the adult. He cannot have the same feelings the adult has regarding his education nor the same justification for a sense of outrage. Because the child often does not know if or how his education may not be a good one, he cannot even be prejudiced against faculty, administration, or anyone else. It is only by a viewing of adult behavior that he can develop these prejudices. For the young student, the line between violence and other physical persuasions such as boycott, strike, or disregarding the law is a fuzzy one. The message he seems to receive is that if you do not like something, act. While a strike or a boycott or a disregarded injunction may be an appropriate procedure for a group of adults with a grievance, the youngster may see such procedures as the green light for disorganized, tumultuous activity. He does not see adult maneuverings as planned strategy, and he may then use violence either as a distorted, imitative action, or because it seems fun, or even in an unfocused attempt to relieve some of the tension he feels about him.

Violence as Lure

Another view of violence concerns its seductive quality and raises the question: What is the lure of violence? Man discovered long ago that violent acts excited him. This is physiologically valid. When one participates in violent acts, either actively or as an observer, there are elevations in blood pressure, heart rate, and respiration rate. These bodily changes are stimulating to the individual, particularly so if juxtaposed to the physiology of an inhibited, bored, or indifferent individual.

Unconsciously, perhaps, man learned how to escape from

what he felt as the humdrum of life by involving himself in the hunt, in war games, in warfare, and in forms of violence that gave him a feeling of involvement and satisfaction. According to this reasoning, it is not violence per se but a sense of aliveness that man, with his capacity and need for feeling, is always seeking.

The forms in which man finds a sense of aliveness are usually accidental. If, as a young child, he finds it through academic learning, then he may provide himself with that satisfaction all of his life. If he finds it with games, sports, music, or art, these may serve to satisfy him. If he achieves it with sex, this may remain his primary avenue for satisfaction. And if he achieves it with acts of violence, these will be lifesaving for him in a figurative sense, because only such acts will make him feel most alive. Just as the act of creativity is exciting and rewarding, so may an act of violence be exciting and satisfying. These outcomes, together with a strong need for social change, tend to make the use of violence a powerful, sometimes irresistible force.

CHAPTER XVI

Working with Patients' Parents

Every Parent Does His Best

Every parent does his best in the rearing of his children. That best may be very poor by an absolute standard. Nevertheless, it is *his* best. No parent tries deliberately to be a poor parent, even when he is unquestionably so. That belief is a *must* for the therapist who has to work with a youngster's (child's, adolescent's or young adult's) parent. Holding that belief is helpful in dislodging a feeling of disdain (overt or covert) for the well-intentioned, but bumblin; ignorant, inept, disinterested, indecisive, conflicted, hosit, unkind, cruel, or otherwise pathogenic parent with whom the therapist has to work.

Disdain is often all too clearly evident in exchanges between therapist and parent. Frequently, it is well hidden from the parent in direct conversation; but it is quickly exposed during a conference, or even during a casual conversation relating to your child-patient's family. In treating a youngster, one is usually obliged to work with the family. It is important, therefore, to deal with the element of disdain early in one's work. One reason for this is the adverse effect such a feeling has upon the child one is trying to help.

Whose Rebellion

One often finds the therapist's position paralleling that of the adolescent patient who seems to be doing well in treatment, but rears up intolerably against his parents. It is common to invest this outcome with psychiatric sanctions, by a statement that the youngster had been previously squashed by his parents and never had a chance to rebel "normally." (I wonder if rebellion is ever normal, except in a political sense. If rebellion means growing with gradually increasing independence, self-sufficiency and ability to assume responsibility for one's self, then let it be so stated. To call that development a rebellion hardly describes what the healthy youngster undergoes in the process of maturing.)

At any rate, the so-called normal rebellion is so heartily encouraged by some therapists that one wonders if the latter is not struggling with some problem of his own; and if, in a kind of turnabout, he is not feeling hostile toward the parents of his patient and is using the patient to emerge vindictively triumphant over the "bad" parents. (Please don't toss this off as a form of countertransference, or you may not stay to scrutinize what I am describing in terms of your own feelings in the particular situation.)

The therapist needs to be neither verbal about nor even conscious of this entire involvement; if his thoughts and feelings veer in the direction I am describing, the patient senses them unconsciously, and is happy to accommodate the therapist by acting out the latter's suppressed negative feelings. Quite often, this kind of worker responds happily to the patient's report that he really "created quite an explosion at home" by his various carryings-on. (This discussion applies as well to spouses or others in close relationships.) The patient is so pleased to have won the obvious approval of his therapist as well as good-natured hurrahs, that he will enter again into the fray and really razzle those old parents! Such an approach, however, may not be at all beneficial and may lead to termination of therapy. This is not to say that such a method may not have its usefulness. But it must be used in an objectively calculated manner, and not to meet the unresolved needs of the professional involved.

This sequence may also take place on the initiation of the patient without any assistance from the therapist. In that case, therapist intervention must be pertinent to existing facts, because the patient, often one of irrational extremes, cannot break away from a position of repressed or suppressed fear, rage, and hostility. Initially, he can move only in the direction of irrational opposites and extremes, in order to dislodge a *set* of nonassertiveness and failure that he had fashioned for himself. The therapist's skill often determines the extremes to which such a patient may go.

One's interest in the occurrence of such events, explosive or not, need not set the patient off on a quest to win bigger and better victories over those "baddies." Just as the therapist's neurotic need may influence the patient's behavior, so can his sincere interest in the facts and feelings of his patient's existence. Facts of "explosive behavior" are often related forthrightly, even if exaggeratedly. Although underlying feelings are more complicated, the patient can nevertheless be engaged in a careful investigation of existing convolutions. He may feel a sense of vindication, which is not surprising in view of his sense of martyrdom with respect to his parents.

But a patient who has not "rebelled" before, and who is proud of being a "good child," may be thrown into immediate conflict. He cannot maintain a position of good child with all of its rewards, which he has no wish to relinquish, and yet all the while enjoy his position of victory over his parents. He knows himself as the good child. To veer toward a position of victory, at the expense of parents' feelings, is to be another person in his own eyes.

He has not learned that one need not always act one way

(good child) or another (assertive child), and that spontaneous responses depend upon specific context. One laughs at a
joke, but one cries at a loss. To be totally consistent would
require only laughter or tears for both. Yet consistency here
is clearly inappropriate. Sometimes a person caught in an
unexpected situation says, "I don't know what to feel,"
realizing that his usual responses are not appropriate to this
new situation, but unable to permit whatever true feelings
he has to surface. The neurotic person cannot make
pertinent moves easily without feeling guilty and coerced.
Thus, the youngster who is rebellious, relevant or not, appropriate or not, feels conflicted because he is departing
from patterns of consistency and predictability that he has
striven to construct for the maintenance of a sense of safety.

Your Problem

If a patient has been led to the point of rebelliousness, his
therapist may not have done him a service. The resulting
sense of self-disapproval, of conflict, and of anxiety may not
necessarily serve the patient at that point. Only in the hands
of an experienced therapist can patient conflict and anxiety
be adequately managed. Even then, it may preclude the
possibility of effective treatment.

It is usually of greater value to the patient to be led to a
point of so-called rebellion by a therapist who is as deeply
concerned for the "impossible" parent as for the patient.
Here there is no risk of the patient fighting the therapist's
battles. Rather. as he approaches that point with his parents
where he must assert himself (assertiveness is not rebelliousness) the patient engages only in his own interest. He is
not to be made in any way responsible for the therapist's
problem with assertiveness. Thus, the patient is not as likely
to create situations in the home which, if allowed to continue, would prove intolerable to both patient and family. The
creation of such situations is one of the pitfalls into which the
inexperienced therapist falls, and he is puzzled when the

patient decides to leave therapy. The therapist may blandly place such a response into a wastebasket labeled "resistances," and he may not be able to view it as behavior critical (at the moment) to the patient's survival, about which the patient is more concerned than the therapist. More commonly, it is the family which has reached the breaking point, and acts to subvert the treatment, or to demand its termination. The worker then must consciously attempt not to influence his patient against a parent or spouse by any word, deed, expression, or inference, because (as explained) he may further burden the patient.

"Impossible" Parent

It is not so much the vocabulary used in describing a parent that is the factor revealing the worker's disdain, contempt, impatience, or dislike. When a worker says that a parent is "impossible" he means that a parent is the poorest possible parent from his viewpoint, and he may be quite accurate in his judgment. Some persons *are* absolutely "impossible parents"—let us make no mistake about that. But rarely does the impossible parent regard himself as such. He is not only a *possible* parent, but more than possible—he actually is a parent. Therefore, whether we believe he is possible or impossible is totally irrelevant. And this is the truth with which we must work in our confrontation with him. To antagonize him in any way is to arouse his defenses, and to directly undermine our own work with him and with our patient.

Having established that he is not only a parent, but possibly the only parent, one may proceed to the next step. That step entails a consideration of all the factors in his personality and background which make him so "impossible," as well as those qualities which can be developed to help him to be more "possible." As already discussed, he may be disinterested, impatient, conflicted, physically or mentally ill, hostile, rejecting, unkind, and even cruel and murderous.

Anything he is or does is existential, and therefore, by definition, possible. The question of how the parent of a battered child could be so cruel is easily answered. He could be so cruel just the way he was so cruel. Whether one watches him being cruel, which would be informing ourselves graphically, or whether one knows of his cruelty by hearsay, it does not change the how-could-he. He could *just that way—the way he did it.* Of course, the question (how-could-he) is not really a question at all; it is an implied accusation: What a terrible thing you have done and what a terrible person you must be.

Conflicts

Making such an inference does not help one in work with a young patient and family. It not only expresses profound disapproval, disgust, or horror, but what is most significant is that it adds a further conflict to an already over-burdened parent. For, regardless of the rationalization for his behavior (and it may be a well-constructed one), a parent in that position usually does feel some measure of guilt. In that context the feeling of guilt would be a symptom of an inner conflict regarding his parental behavior. Two common opposing forces in this conflict are activated: one is a sense of righteousness for doing his duty as a parent, even though he incurs his child's displeasure or even hatred while in the performance of that worthy act; and the other is a sense of self-disapproval and self-dislike for being a despicable person, and for being so unkind to his own child.

These simultaneous, opposing values are clearly irreconcilable. Because the individual is not aware of those inner workings, he is left only with a sense of guilt, which can be an uncomfortable and even intolerable condition. That condition can seriously hamper the possibility of improvement in his role as parent, for the parent is then driven to relieve himself of his guilt, rather than attend to the various, realistic demands of parenthood. The need for relief from this opposition creates distortions in other activities of living. If the parent cannot relieve himself, he may become even more irritable, impatient, tired, and anxious. This may lead to additional destructive parental activities.

Even in the psychopathic, sadistic parent, who has manifested cruelty to the extreme, and who, it is maintained, experiences no conflict or anxiety, one finds the exhortation of how-could-you responded to with but more of the same. Why he does this can be only an assumption on our part unless he tells us this directly, which he is not likely to do. The most we can obtain from him is the rationalization, "It is my duty to raise my child properly and I must do it by whatever means I think best," or, "I can't stand him (the child), and I don't want to be bothered by him. So he has to learn to behave," or, "He has to know who's boss." or some such variation. The assumption is that this parent does experience anxiety and can insure its alleviation only by (1) repeated forays into the kinds of familiar behavior he has developed as a way of life, or by (2) strengthening that "good parent" rationale, throwing weight onto one side of his conflict (that of being a dutiful parent). The impasse created by opposing forces is overcome and the weakening of one of the attractions affords him some relief. As in a tug of war, as soon as one side weakens, the struggle is resolved. For the psychotherapist to set the parent's conflict into action by a remark of implied disapproval may serve to invite more of the same poor behavior, which will most likely be directed against the youngster we are trying to help or protect.

It is sufficient to know of their existence; we need not become involved with those extremes of parental behavior because they are not the most common conditions we shall encounter. The parent we encounter most frequently is one whose sense of external disapproval and guilt is consciously stirred. This sets into motion an inner conflict, as described earlier, regarding his basic feelings about himself. Involvement in that conflict generates feelings of anxiety in the parent. He cannot tolerate the anxiety, and must resort to his own particular ploys to relieve himself. Like those of the more disturbed parent, his tactics may include the kinds of behavior already found by the worker to be so damaging to the youngster. But neither does this parent have any other recourse. He would if he could—this point cannot be emphasized too strongly. If he were free to do something else he might do it. If he has not done something constructive that the worker feels to be self-evident, it is because it is not self-evident to the parent.

Even when the parent has thought of another approach, he may feel that he is incapable of actualizing it. There is great distance between the thought and deed; the thought may be "the father of the deed," but just as father is certainly not son, the thought is certainly not the deed.

Inertia

This is the hollow in which many parents find themselves. "I know I should do this—or that," they cry; then they thrash about because of an inertia which they explain as some kind of unique inability to be other than they are. There is nothing unique or even unusual about the situation. What's done is done and similarly, what's not done is not done. Thinking and wanting are essential to the act, but they are not enough. Nothing is done that is not done. One will not, without assistance, be able to get up from his chair and walk across the room unless he moves his body in certain ways, directly toward the goal he desires.

The necessity of doing what might be done to improve a relationship is not understood well enough. Parents just wait for something to "happen." It sometimes does, and if it happens frequently enough, the parent is deprived of the opportunity to be the initiator of the circumstances of his life. He is then completely at the mercy of whatever external factors impinge upon his existence. If those external factors are favorable (i.e., supportive family, helpful friends, accepting friends, cooperative children, etc.,) he is fortunate. If they are unfavorable, he will be buffeted about, incapable of contributing to his life's progress.

It is at this point that the therapist's intervention becomes relevant. He might do well to keep in mind the following simple points when he approaches the parent. If the parent has not thought of something first, he cannot do it. If he has not the experience to do something, he cannot do it. If he has not the necessary information, he cannot do it. Lastly, if the parent could do better, he would. At any given moment, he is doing *his* very best. It will become one of the responsibilities of the therapist to provide him with information and with the idea of self-activation toward a desired goal.

Optimism Helps

That is a very brief sampling of one type of approach the worker may employ. However, this frame of reference must not be allowed to discourage the worker, nor excuse him from making all necessary efforts to help the parent. Basically, this reference is used to establish the facts, without which the worker would be handicapped. He must know how ignorant, how inept, how disinterested, or how informed, apt, and interested the parent is. Only then can he determine which efforts might prove most beneficial. At no time need the worker doubt the sincerity of the parent. And to whatever degree both therapist and parent can remain optimistic about improvement in the relationship, it is so much better for their continuing work together.

If the parent is indeed disinterested or ignorant and unaware, he cannot be regarded as insincere. If he is aware of his inadequacies as a parent it will prove of no value to either him or the worker to have it brought to his attention. Two results of such "truthfulness" are predictable: (1) the parent must defend himself and therefore become closed off to the worker's intervention, and (2) the worker loses valuable time, in which he might utilize a variety of other techniques for helping the patient. A less common outcome is a sense of discouragement and, possibly, a depression in the parent who feels helpless to change the quality of his relating toward his child. This is a phase which is, however, almost unavoidable in a parent involved in an intense search (by psychoanalysis) for the motives which direct his outward behavior. The psychotherapists being addressed here do not have the background for that type of involvement. Even if they do have adequate training and experience, this is not the occasion for the application of techniques used in depth analysis.

Watch Your Biases

If the goal is to diminish tensions which make for poor relationships, the therapist works with the parent to find alternative approaches to the child. Should the parent have to be harsh and unkind, then that is the best he can do, even though we recognize that it is deplorable to be harsh and unkind. Any standards, ours or anyone else's, are irrelevant to the issue. This does not mean that we approve of how he acts, but neither do we disapprove. What does it mean to approve or disapprove of blue or brown eyes? It certainly would not change anything. We are merely trying to describe that which confronts us, phenomenologically, rather than judgmentally. The phenomenological is the position, I believe, of Supreme Court justices. Their function is to describe or make explicit the meaning inherent in the law, not to judge the worth or value of the explications. Justice, it seems, deals with the guilt or innocence of the defendent only in terms of the meaning of the law.

While we are not interested in anyone's guilt or innocence, the therapist must have something of the quality of the Supreme Court justice; he must have the facts described for himself and he must accept them as such without prejudice. He may say to himself, "This parent is a rotten parent," in the same descriptive sense that he states, "This parent is six feet tall." If he were to state, "My God, this parent is six feet tall!" with certain inflections, it would be the same as stating, "My God, but this parent is a rotten parent!" The prejudice is clearly in evidence in the two latter examples and absent, by tone, manner, expression, in the former ones. The former statements establish facts. The latter statements establish facts and the worker's particular bias regarding those facts. Naturally, the worker has a particular system of values; but it is well to appreciate both its irrelevance to this kind of work, and its destructiveness for the parent whom one is supposed to be helping. Furthermore, the therapist has to work to gradually and eventually set his biases to rest in his work with patients as well as their parents.

The next question which arises is: How can you be so unbiased, so objective, so accepting of various human characteristics as to remain tranquil in the face of a very poor family situation? The point is that you are *not* unbiased, objective, etc. You will often feel disturbed, angry, indignant, etc. But the more unbiased you are the more helpful you are to the parent and/or child you are treating. This does not mean that one should encourage damaging behavior on the part of the parent. But clearly identifying a tendency toward bias, practicing techniques for developing nonjudgmental attitudes, and, finally, appreciating the basic worth of such an approach will work toward the development of a well-grounded attitude in this context, and a belief in the premise that each parent is indeed doing his best, whatever that best may be. Working to rid oneself of biases is a life-long work. So don't have any great expectations for a while!

Her Duty

The following is an example of the manner in which a worker proceeded when he heard of a particularly damaging exchange between a mother and her child. The woman is a person who prides herself on her concern for her children, believing that children must not be "spoiled" and must be helped to develop responsibility for themselves. She therefore takes her motherhood very seriously and devotes most of her time to assiduous care of her family. On one occasion of recalcitrance in her child, this woman revealed she had scolded and beaten him and, finally, threatened to "burn his hands in the oven." The therapist's response of silent shock was followed by the thought, "How could anyone burn somebody else's hands in the oven without burning his own hands in the process? Surely, the child would not be sitting there quietly while his hands were being burned!" The therapist remarked that it was entirely clear that this woman's first concern was to rear her child in ways that she thought were "proper." The woman accepted that statement as a compliment and a truth. Any suggestion of attack by word, tone, or expression would have "turned her off" and the therapeutic intent might have come to naught. Since no defensiveness was aroused in her, she went on to explain how a mother's first duty to her children was to teach them how to behave. It was obvious that her goal justified her means.

Questioned on the effectiveness of her method, the parent admitted that it was not effective. In the following exchange it became clear that the child felt neglected; an elder child with a chronic disease received the bulk of attention from the rest of the family. It was suggested to the mother that she might spend just a little time each week, perhaps fifteen or thirty minutes, with the neglected child, devoting that time exclusively to him. The woman was able to accept that suggestion as an alternative to her cruelly punitive method. If the therapist had initially expressed disdain or other negative feelings, this woman would have closed herself off from such an alternative.

Closing off the parent is not what we are after, if we expect to be of service to our patient. But I'm not referring only to not expressing feelings of dismay or disgust. I am

suggesting that these feelings may not arise if we can remember that the parent's intention is to help and not harm
his child. Of course we know that the "road to hell is paved
with good intentions." Our task, therefore, is to try to effect
change in the *outcome* and not in the good intentions. They
cannot be improved upon, as far as the parent is concerened.
Don't bother with that; keep yourself unimpeded by your
negative response as effectively as you can, so you can give
the parent various tools with which to work in a new approach to his child. That is where your obligation lies, not in
chastisement.

CHAPTER XVII
Find the Good Life

New Goals

The beginning psychotherapist may occasionally have the opportunity to work with a selected patient over an extended period of time. His interest and goals may shift from symptom relief, organization of basic life functioning, and discharge to include helping the patient become more aware of unconscious impediments.

Providing the occasion for the patient's discovery of aspects of himself is an essential feature of long-term therapy. This can be accomplished when the therapist does not intrude himself too frequently or at an untimely moment. When the therapist wishes to intervene, so that the patient can pause with himself, this can be accomplished by speaking very briefly; more than ten words at any single intervention are probably too many. Most therapists become aware of this, sooner or later; but it must be said with regard to our ever-present limitations, that some are totally incapable of practicing such restraint.

Pause

Effectiveness of intervention depends upon the therapist's helping his patient to *pause* at the very moment that they are sharing. This moment is free of the burden, responsibility, or distraction of the next moment to come, and of the preceding one—or, in broader terms, of the future and of the past. To the extent that such a pause may occur during a session, it is possible that it may occur again elsewhere, to a lesser degree.

The following is an example of *attending to the moment* with a middle-aged, financially and professionally successful lawyer, who was born and reared in comfortable circumstances in a small Southern town. He attended schools there and then made his way East to settle down to marriage and a career with an established, conservative, highly respected law firm. His life had been an orderly and productive one.

The patient entered treatment because of insomnia and mounting tension. Although he wanted to cooperate, he found it difficult to see himself in the role of patient. He had the kind of background that demanded, however, that he be proper at all times, so he made every effort to be the "good patient." So hard did he try that he was consistently appreciative and agreeable, something that made it difficult for him to be free in his associations.

Mental Fatigue

Upon one occasion he entered the office, smiled broadly, sat down and said: "I would like to know what happened here last time."

"What are you referring to?"

"Last week when I was here I had had a very hard day at the office. I was just beat when I arrived. When I came away, I felt quite relaxed, and I want to know how it happened."

"Can you tell me something about your feeling of relaxation?"

"Well, I felt awfully tired when I came—not physically tired, really, but a sort of mental fatigue."

"And what happened?"

"That I can't tell you, because I have no idea—not the slightest—how it came about. I've thought about it a great deal, and yet I can't come up with anything."

"Is it last week you are referring to?"

"Yes, that's when I came in feeling mentally exhausted."

Here the patient began to repeat some of the things he said the previous week. The following are excerpts of that session, with the usual pauses and repetitions. Most of the therapist's remarks follow pauses of the patient and were made with the intention of involving the patient more deeply in whatever he was saying.

"I have been trying to keep up with the pressures at the office. I can hardly keep up with the quantity of demands upon me. There are so many calls to make and so many people to see. And I get the feeling: How am I ever going to crowd all these into the time I have? The effect of all this is so terribly tiring."

"Is that what makes you feel mentally fatigued?"

"Yes."

"Can you tell me what that feeling is?"

"It's a feeling of pressure, not necessarily physical fatigue, because I don't really do anything that would make me tired that way. It's a feeling of having too many things to do."

"I'm not clear about what you're saying."

"After a while I'm aware that I'm trying to separate things and decide which are most important, which can be left until the next day, which people will be the least offended if I don't call them back, and that sort of thing. Through all of this there runs a thread of concern about the consequences."

"Tell me about that thread of concern."

"There's no fear involved, at least not consciously."

"What is there?"

"There's dissatisfaction in not being able to do all that's called for . . . that I've not organized things better so that this accumulation wouldn't take place . . . I don't think about resentment. I'm not aware of any, except maybe that of dissatisfaction that I haven't handled the organization any better."

"Anything else?"

"Perhaps a little impatience—yes, I think so."

"Impatience?"

"The same thing I mentioned before, that I haven't organized better."

"Yes?"

"This could lead to a threatened failure."

"Threatened failure?"

"I mean, in case there was some possibility of a disaster."

This point was not at all clear. Eventually the patient described his state of mind as he went through this kind of a day, in which there was much too much to be done. With the therapist trying to understand what the patient's "mental fatigue" consisted of, the patient was questioned further because he seemed willing to let it go at merely a label, assuming that both knew what he meant.

Arranging

Up to this point it had been established that some of the elements of his "mental fatigue" were (1) the pressure to do more things than he could handle; (2) dissatisfaction with the organization of his time; (3) impatience at his performance; (4) resentment directed at himself; (5) possible fear of consequences which could be detrimental to him or to one of his clients. The patient stated that he had not thought there could be so many feelings or facets to his mental fatigue. He wondered if there were not "a lot more" and felt that it was all very complicated. He was questioned about the thoughts and feelings he has when he is at his desk, trying to get through his day's work.

"I try to arrange in proper order those things that I have to do so that I can attend to the most pressing ones first."

"What do you do then?"

"I go through the list. If I have ten things to do, I try to take care of one, two, and three first. Then I go on to four, five, and six, and so on. But at the same time that I'm thinking about one, I'm trying to figure out how I can do the others, how to avoid certain ones, how to delay others.''

"You mean that while you're attending to one, you're thinking about the others as well?''

"Yes, and sometimes I hold my head and feel that it's all just too much. I feel I just can't think any more. This is what I mean by mental fatigue.''

"You're thinking about one, two, three, four, five, six simultaneously?''

"Yes, I can't get the whole business out of my head, not even the things that I've already done. I'm thinking about them, too. How I handled them, that maybe I should have done this or that.''

"So you're trying to attend to all of them at once? The ones you did, the ones you're doing, and the ones you're going to do?''

"Yes, I have them all on my mind at the same time. I don't know how that's possible, but that's the way it seems to be.''

"No wonder you're tired.''

Distractions

Next an attempt was made to find out how he might feel without such a task, and whether or not there was a connection among the items. His answer was that there might sometimes be a connection between them, but that most of the time there was none.

"But even if there is a connection, I keep going back and forth between what I did, what I'm going to do, and what I am doing. It's a terrible distraction.''

"Do these distractions interfere with what you're doing at any single moment?''

"Yes, they keep me from concentrating on what is right in front of me. I do concentrate, and I do get a lot done, I admit, but I'm also concentrating on the other things.''

"Do you feel that this impedes your effectiveness in any way?''

"I've never thought about that, but it would seem that it

would have to. I've never even thought about what I've been doing. It just comes to me as I talk about it. And I think that what it does is to make me more tense.''

''Is mental fatigue associated with actual mental work you have to do in situations which confront you, one after the other?''

Mental Activity

At that point, the patient began to speak of mental activity in other contexts—at meetings and at luncheons and dinners with prominent persons of the legal and financial worlds. He described the intense quality of mental activity that accompanied these occasions. He told how stimulating and exciting they were to him, and how they left him with a feeling of exhilaration and well-being, ''like a rub-down after a good tennis match—tingling alive.''

''No feeling of mental fatigue?''

''No; in fact, just the opposite.''

''Yet you describe intense mental work in relation to situations with possible far-reaching effects.''

''Yes, and yet there's no feeling of either physical or mental fatigue.''

''What's the difference between this kind of thinking and the thinking that you describe in the office, which makes you feel mentally fatigued?''

To this the patient replied that in the former situations he felt that the demands of the moment caused him to be exceedingly attentive. Then he said that he never knew just what was going to be said, what might develop, and so was not busy worrying if anything would be completed, for he could not have stated which point came before which other point.

''In the office there's this feeling of dissatisfaction with myself that I'm not better organized, and there's my annoyance with myself. I don't have any of this at all, at these meetings.''

"What happens with the distraction of what went before and what comes after?"

"It's all part of the same thing. I'm still a little worried about what I have done and what I'm going to do."

"Is there any difference between this distraction and the distraction in the office?"

"There seems to be. At the meetings, I just don't feel the dissatisfaction I feel at the office."

"Is it possible that the absence of time pressure permits you to be distracted more comfortably? In other words, you have the time at your disposal. But when you're more rushed, you have no time to waste and so you feel the pinch more acutely."

He laughed: "That may be so. It certainly makes sense."

No Rush

It then came out that the feeling of dissatisfaction with himself was the direct antecedent of the mental fatigue which was, in fact, a logy, heavy feeling of depression to which this man could hardly admit. He was reminded of his initial question about wanting to know how he had been "transformed" the week before. Some of what he had said was reviewed for him, ending with "and then you came in here feeling as you did." He tried to describe what had been said in that hour. As a common denominator, he felt that there had been no sense of rush, no sense of time pressure, no sense of deliberate planning or direction.

In the above productions, several other courses might have been followed. The matter of organization was one possibility, because to organize effectively is exactly what this man has been trying to do with his entire life and with everyone related to it. His greatest dissatisfaction is that it does not come off. But it was felt that to talk about "organization" *per se*, at that moment, might be too global and a distraction. For that reason, the feeling of mental fatigue was pursued.

This patient was able to be attentive to the very moment before him. Even when talking about memories of the past, there was a presentness about it; he enjoyed remembering things which he had not thought about in decades. His pleasure in remembering and in retelling was communicated to the therapist, who was interested not only in what he was saying, but who was also responding to him as he recalled.

When current matters were discussed in the session, the quality of interest on the part of the patient, as of the therapist, was immediate. The patient wanted to be there to understand, to be able to make use of what was presented. He was not hampered by the usual distraction that he visited upon himself.

Distraction by the past and future makes the present burdensome and therefore fatiguing. As he said, "It is too much. I want to stop." The responsibility of dealing with present, past, and future simultaneously, indeed, is too great a burden for anyone to bear.

The patient left this second hour feeling that the relaxation he had experienced in the previous hour was the result of his being able to relieve himself, for even a short time, of a need to attend to everything at one moment, and instead, to attend to the immediacy of a single issue. Similarly the vignette presented here is a single moment in an unbroken string of such moments. Each one can be examined alone, yet in a broad context.

Back to Center

What this man was able to do was not only *not* fatiguing but, on the contrary, actually had a nourishing quality. It had been a time of connectedness with himself. During the previous hour he had also talked of his boyhood on a Southern farm—of doing chores, of his mother doing her baking in an iron stove, of tantalizingly delicious odors, of walks in the woods, of picking wild flowers, of swimming in the pond, of being in a cornfield and seeing straight rows of corn in every direction.

During his lifetime this man has departed from the center of his being. The memory of homey, personal details possibly contributes to his coming closer to that center which seems to have resided in him as a boy. The existence of that center is probably what has made possible the pleasure and satisfaction he has experienced through the years with respect to his work and the contribution he feels he has made in his field.

The session he spoke of was one in which he had been invited to take a closer look at himself. This was done in two ways. One was in a confrontation with what he was actually doing and feeling during his moments of stress. Although it was painful for him to look at himself, he did grasp himself in a way he had not done previously.

The second was through the memory of simple joys of boyhood, where his love of nature was what it still is to this day, a source of comfort and tranquility. This, too, was a confrontation of his feeling. In this instance, however, it was not a confrontation causing pain and perhaps growth, but had a quality of peace and of gentleness. A question might be raised here: Are moments of gentle confrontation as significant and perhaps as therapeutic as those which are fraught with turmoil and dismay?

CHAPTER XVIII

A Note on Karen Horney

In her many works, Dr. Karen Horney repeatedly refers to the neurotic character structure, rather than to psychosis. Nevertheless, it is the belief of her followers that a grounding in Horney theory is as useful in treatment of the psychoses as it is for the neuroses.

There is a qualitative distinction to be made between psychosis and neurosis. Psychosis is more likely the outcome of exorbitant anxiety present in the very young and potentially psychotic individual. An anxiety which is overpowering in its presence, it drives the child to develop defenses of a qualitatively different order. Yet, despite dramatic differences, general outlines of those defenses derive from similar matrices. But propensity to distort defenses out of all recognition renders them unfamiliar and bizarre to the therapist who is rooted in the ordinary.

The beginning trainee may gain immediately if he sees that the syptomatology and defenses of psychotic patients are not totally different from those of the neurotic patient. However, an insupportable anxiety, together with other unremitting schizophrenogenic factors, eventually leads to psychosis and schizophrenic development.

Ideally, self-realization occurs as a natural, spontaneous process in all human beings. That is, given his physical, intellectual, cultural, and experiential resources, each individual may realize a unique potential in his own particular way. That development could lead to a state of well-being and a sense of satisfaction with one's chosen path. That is a basic tenet of Karen Horney's theory of neurosis.

As a "special form of human development which is the antithesis of healthy growth," the neurotic process so pre-occupies an individual that he often loses sight of himself as an authentic being, and subverts his development to his need for safety. Rather than viewing the world as a vast, glorious arena in which to flex and experience himself in all respects, he sees the world as potentially threatening, and one in which he feels isolated and helpless. Such a view leads him to the elaboration, on both conscious and un-conscious levels, of a psychological edifice, designed to protect. That structure is referred to as the neurotic character structure. Depending upon one's intelligence, vitality, imagination, and resourcefulness, the structure is more or less complex and effective; but it is always a failure in terms of the creator's sense of well-being.

Failure is understandable when one considers that the major work of neurosis has to do with constant vigilance against real or imagined attacks. Even if those attacks are successfully repulsed, the belief that there is always another lurking behind can never lead to a sense of security or a state of tranquility.

Neurotic development is, clearly and simply, a protective device—a must—to counter anticipated threats from all sides. That explains the difficulty a therapist may encounter when he "attacks" defenses. Such an attack must be viewed by the neurotic individual as an attempt to strip him of his protections and to leave him quivering, a jelly-like mass, exposed to the terrible vicissitudes of life. He cannot permit that. The beginning therapist must therefore not expect to make inroads in breaching the patient's defenses. It is only when the patient regards his original premise as invalid that his defenses may become obsolete. Such obsolescence is not to be expected in the psychoses, where, at best, a diminishing of anxiety makes the rigidity of defenses less imperative.

In describing maturation of the neurotic character

structure, Karen Horney used the ordinary manner in which people grow as her point of reference. She classified three ways of being: growing toward people, away from people, and against people. These common forms of development may be regarded as neurotic only when they become compulsive.

In a healthy human relationship the moves toward, against, or away from others are not mutually exclusive. The ability to want and to give affection, to give in, the ability to be assertive or to fight, and the ability to keep to oneself—these are complementary capacities for good human relations. But in the child who feels himself on precarious ground because of his basic anxiety, these moves become extreme and rigid. Affection, for instance, becomes clinging; compliance becomes appeasement and self-effacement. Similarly, he is driven to rebel or to keep aloof, without reference to his real feelings and regardless of the inappropriateness of his attitude in a particular situation. The degree of blindness and rigidity in his attitudes is in proportion to the intensity of the basic anxiety lurking within him.

A quality of compulsiveness underlies every aspect of neurosis, and is inseparable from neurosis. To be compulsive in any respect is to be neurotic in that respect. Compulsiveness encompasses more than so-called compulsions in which, for example, one follows a ritual or uses some form of repetitious activity to allay anxiety.

In Horney's formulation, the *real self* refers to that central inner force, common to all human beings and yet unique in each, that is the source of natural, healthy development and is implicit in the potential of one's genetic and individual nature. Horney likened this concept to an acorn and oak tree. Given the opporunity, the intrinsic potentialities of the acorn will develop into the oak.

The neurotic individual has difficulty developing self-confidence or an accurate sense of self. His strength is sapped by constantly having to be on the defensive. Nonetheless, he requires some sense of identity and of self-confidence, or a substitute for them. In striving for a substitute, he feels he must raise himself above others in order to achieve any feeling of self-worth. As soon as that practice begins, he also sets into motion a process of alienation through elaboration of an *idealized image*. By this means, he silences all feelings and thoughts which do not, in his opinion, contribute both to his protection and aggrandizement. His search for a feeling of identity is fulfilled spuriously through his imagination. He unconsciously and gradually creates in his mind an image of himself that will serve many or even all of the activities of life. This image often has unlimited power and exalted faculties. It is called "the comprehensive neurotic solution."

Energy and vitality driving toward self-realization are thus shifted toward the aim of actualizing the idealized self or, at least, of keeping from awareness the gulf between one's actual self and one's image of self. Pursuit of this "search for glory" knows of no respite; the moment the drive subsides, the neurotic person must confront his actual self, which he finds intolerable in comparison to his imaginary ideal. Other elements inherent in the search for glory, besides a central self-idealization, are an unrelenting competitiveness, a pressing need for perfection, neurotic ambition, and absolute vindication.

These then are the pathetic and self-defeating occupations to which every neurotic person is chained—to a greater or lesser degree. Demanding, draining, and totally engrossing occupations, they serve to dilute and scatter qualities of humaneness, spontaneity, and joy like so many tumbleweeds drifting across an arid and barren human spirit, rendered incapable of relishing its inherent richness.

Index